CRITICAL THINKING

The Beginners User Manual to Improve Your Communication and Self Confidence Skills Everyday.

The Tools and The Concepts for Problem Solving and Decision Making.

Table of Contents

CRITICAL THINKING   1

TABLE OF CONTENTS   3

INTRODUCTION   7

CHAPTER ONE: HOW TO DEVELOP SKILLS IN CRITICAL
THINKING   10

CHAPTER TWO: BENEFITS OF CRITICAL THINKING   53

CHAPTER THREE: ROUTINES TO IMPROVE CRITICAL THINKING
                                                                65

CHAPTER FOUR: TECHNIQUES, STRATEGIES, SKILLS   89

CHAPTER FIVE: TYPES OF CRITICAL THINKING   102

CHAPTER SIX: EXERCISES FOR CRITICAL THINKING   111

CHAPTER SEVEN: CRITICAL THINKING VERSUS NON-CRITICAL
THINKING   123

CONCLUSION   145

purview. There are no scenarios in which the publisher or the original author of this work can be in any fashion deemed liable for any hardship or damages that may befall them after undertaking information described herein.

Additionally, the information in the following pages is intended only for informational purposes and should thus be thought of as universal. As befitting its nature, it is presented without assurance regarding its prolonged validity or interim quality. Trademarks that are mentioned are done without written consent and can in no way be considered an endorsement from the trademark holder.

Introduction

Congratulations on buying *Critical Thinking* and thank you for doing so!

Have you ever been faced with an important situation that required your decision-making skill—or have you been faced with a problem that your answer or solution to it was very important not only to yourself but to others—then, in such moments, you panic and wonder what to do? Well, panic no more!

This book starts by discussing what critical thinking is and its benefits as well as why it is important to have critical thinking skills in your everyday life. You will learn how to analyze problems critically and use the critical thinking process to find solutions to your challenges—whether you are a parent, a student, a worker, or even a leader.

The book will also discuss how to develop skills in critical thinking, its benefits, routines to improve it, its underlying techniques or strategies, and its different types. This book will also include exercises to help you think critically and also practice your critical thinking skills. The book further discusses the obstacles that you are likely to face as you develop your critical thinking skills and the ways to overcome them so that critical thinking becomes next to nature.

The book also analyzes in detail the characteristics of a critical thinker and the skills that you as a reader need to cultivate if you want to become one. As you study the book, you will also understand the differences between critical thinking and ordinary thinking as well as the advantages of one over the other—thus giving you reasons as to why you should cultivate critical thinking skills.

You have probably heard the expression, "Look before you leap." Critical thinking is the step right after we look—to assess what we might be leaping into and whether we need to look for a better destination before we jump. It also lets us understand if we really need to jump or not.

There are other books on this subject on the market, so thank you again for choosing this one! Every effort has been made to make sure it is full of as much useful information as possible. Please enjoy!

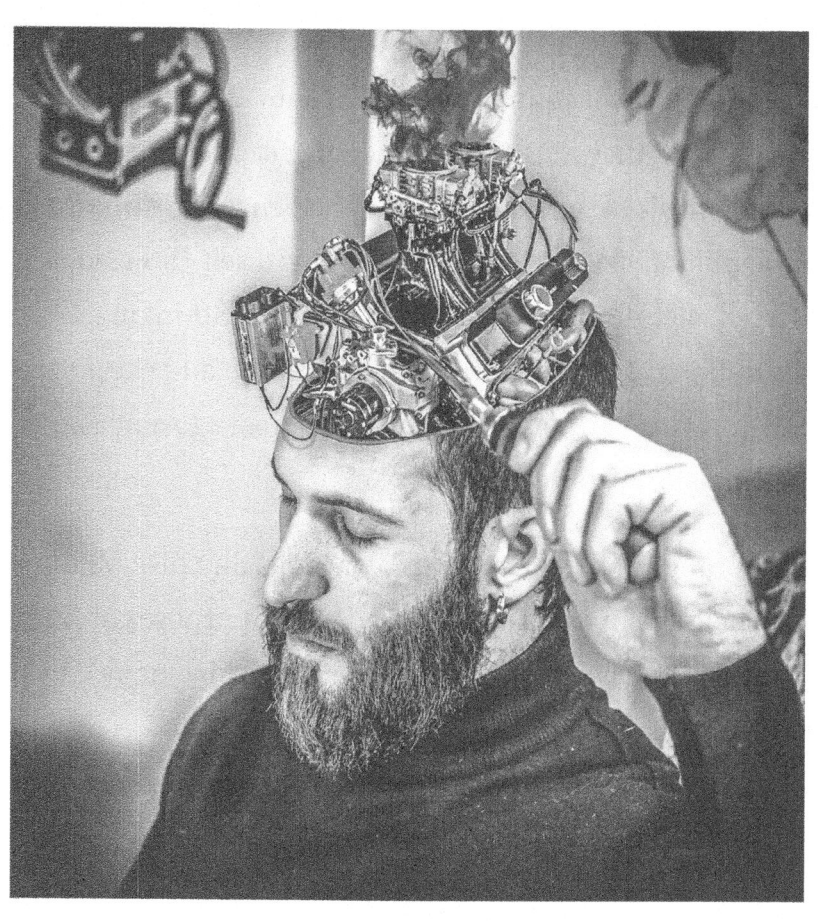

CHAPTER ONE: HOW TO DEVELOP SKILLS IN CRITICAL THINKING

Critical thinking is a complex subject. There are different definitions, but they all generally include skeptical, unbiased, and rational analysis of presented facts or evidence. Critical thinking is very individualized in the sense that it is a self-directed, self-monitored, self-disciplined, and self-corrective thinking. It involves effective and efficient communication and excellent problem-solving skills as commitment against egocentrism and socio-centrism.

A diverse range of skills, methods, concepts, and disciplines is what is included in critical thinking. For the purposes of this book, we will discuss its characteristics shared by many definitions of it.

What Is Critical Thinking?

Critical thinking can be defined as the ability to clearly think and be rational about your beliefs or what to do. It involves the ability of one to engage in independent and reflective thinking.

A person with critical thinking skills should be able to do the following:

- Objectively reflect on why their beliefs and values are justified;
- Systematically solve problems;
- Understand the connection between ideas logically;
- Identify, construct, understand, and analyze arguments;
- Identify inconsistent mistakes in reasoning; and
- Understand the importance and relevance of ideas.

Critical thinking can also be described as the ability to analyze facts in order to reach a conclusion logically. It involves careful consideration of information established as true, clearly outlining a rational process of thought about that information, and objectively arriving at a judgment.

If that last paragraph sounds complicated, the good news is that you have probably already engaged in some form of critical thinking.

For example, if you want to purchase a new car and if you know what you want in terms of the car's price, condition, quality, and features—you then have to compare several different car models. You might read several reviews about a particular car that seems like the right one. You'll collect more information about that specific car. If it fits your criteria, you'll then compare sellers in terms of their pricing and customer feedback to find a seller that you can trust to give you the right car at a good price. Along the way, you'll make sure that the reviews you are reading come from reliable sources that honestly describe the car and the seller (rather than old reviews that may no longer reflect current conditions, reviews that don't explain anything, or biased reviews that might not reflect an accurate assessment). Once you have analyzed the facts, you find the right car model and seller and ultimately make your purchase.

You just used a form of critical thinking to purchase a car. You had a clear purpose (finding a car), you came up with a solution (you decided which model of car you wanted to buy), you used information (reviews) while carefully determining which information was truthful and useful (only using reviews you trusted), analyzed that information, and solved your problem (you now have a new car).

You did NOT simply pick a car that looked nice in the photographs and went to the first car dealership you found one random day. You also didn't just take every review at face value, or buy a certain car because someone told you to buy that one. You

You not only thought about your decision and used the information to come to it, but you also thought about why you were making that particular choice and put some thought into the information in front of you.

Of course, sifting through all of those reviews, prices, and feedback is time-consuming and not always simple. If you are trying to decide upon which political candidate to vote for, which college you should attend, or some other decision that may involve your own personal values, the process of critical thinking can be even more complex—thus, this book will help you understand critical thinking as a tool for everyday life as well as the "big questions" you may come across.

It is important to note that critical thinking is not about the accumulation of information. If a person has an excellent memory or is aware of many facts, it does not mean that the person is a critical thinker. A critical thinker is that person that is able to realize the consequences from the information they have, and understands how to effectively use the information they have to solve problems and seek more relevant information to stay informed.

Being argumentative or critical of others is now what critical thinking is all about. The skills of critical thinking can be used to point out fallacies and wrong reasoning, play a role in joint reasoning and constructive improvements and tasks. Critical thinking can also be used to improve work processes and enhance social institutions.

It has been argued that critical thinking obstructs creativity because it involves following of the rules of rationality and logic while creativity may involve breaking of the same rules. However, this is not true. Critical thinking is very compatible with many aspects of creative thinking. In essence, critical thinking is an important part of creativity, as we require critical thinking in order to evaluate and enhance creative ideas.

Skills in Critical Thinking

Critical thinking is a lifelong process that even the deepest thinkers continuously practice and refine further. Think about the following skills less like something you can just suddenly perfect and more like habits of mind that you'll always take with you—habits that will improve over time. Regardless of your origin or background, it is extremely important to have critical thinking skills. The lack of such skills can actually break one's career as a result of the inability to understand and analyze information effectively.

In this era of immense competition, critical thinking skills are more important than ever before. According to Kris Potrafka, everything is at risk—thus the need to think more critically. Lack of critical thinking will definitely lessen your chances of climbing the ladder in your career or industry of choice. In order not to succumb to such, it is important to develop your skills in critical thinking. However, it is important first to understand what those skills are in order to know how to improve or enhance them.

There are no universal standards for the skills required in critical thinking, but in this section, we shall discuss six of them:

1. Identification

Firstly, you need to determine what's wrong and what influenced this to happen. Only through understanding your circumstance can you solve your problem.

Once you have identified the problem or situation, you need to stop and take a mental inventory of what is going on as you inquire:

- What is being done?
- What caused your situation?
- What will likely happen?

2. Research

When comparing the different aspects of a situation or an issue, uninfluenced research ability is important. Arguments must be convincing. This means that the figures and facts presented may be lacking in context or are not credible. The best solution in such a case is to perform independent verification, identify the source of information and analyze it.

To help with this, verify the unsourced claims. Is the person bringing the argument offering their source of information? If you ask and there is no clear answer, that should serve as a warning. It is also important to know that not all sources are credible. Learn to verify the sources of any information and their authenticity.

3. Identify biases

This is a difficult skill. It is not easy to recognize a bias yet it is very crucial in critical thinking. Strong critical thinkers must be objective in evaluating the information they receive. Take the assumption that you are a judge required to listen to both sides as well as keeping in mind the biases on both sides.

Of equal importance however if not more, is learning how you must set aside your own biases so that your judgment is impartial. Learn to debate and argue with your own thoughts and perceptions. This is important as a skill because it enables you to see things from different viewpoints.

Always asses your source of information and challenge the evidence that forms your beliefs. You must always be aware of the existence of biases. As you analyze any information or argument, it is important to ask yourself the following questions:

- Who benefits?
- The source of information—is it credible, or does it have a hidden agenda?
- Is the source biased and overlooks details proving them wrong?
- Is it persuasive enough to let make people believe?

4. Inference

The ability to internalize and make conclusions based on available information is also an important skill in mastering critical thinking. Most of the information won't mean as is. As a critical thinker, you will often need to analyze the information presented and come up with conclusions based on raw data.

It is not easy to infer. An inference is an informed guess, and the ability to correctly infer can be enhanced by consciously making an effort to collect as much information as you possibly can before you jump into conclusions. Anytime you are faced with a new situation to evaluate, begin by looking for clues like headlines, featured statistics or images and ask yourself what may be going on based on what you have.

5. Determine Relevance

Critical thinking can be very challenging when it comes to figuring out what information is most relevant to analyze. In many cases, you may be presented with information that may seem very important only to realize that it is a minor point to consider.

The best solution to determine relevance is to by first understanding what is expected. Have you been asked to find a solution? Should you understand the trend? When you understand what is expected out of the situation, it becomes much easier to know what information is relevant and what is not.

Another tip to determining the relevance of information is by making a list of data points that you rank in order of relevance. In doing this, you will likely have a list that includes relevant information at the top of the list and not so important information all the way down. Then, trim down these details and put your attention to what's relevant.

6. Curiosity

It is an easier choice to accept every information presented at face value. However, this can be disastrous when faced with a situation that requires thinking critically. Every human being is naturally curious. Don't allow the impulse to ask questions to die because that is not the way of critical thinkers.

Train yourself to be productively curious. Asking insightful questions about your daily reality necessitates mindfulness, and it's a vital ability you must acquire as a critical thinker.

Facts and Logic

The simplest explanation of critical thinking is that it is your thoughts plus truth. If you take nothing else away from this book, the importance of facts and logic cannot be stressed enough. The most crucial thing you can do to develop as a critical thinker is to support what you think, say, and do with facts, and subject it to logical scrutiny.

As stated earlier, critical thinking is the ability to analyze facts in order to reach a conclusion logically. A fact is a statement that can be supported by external evidence or observable experience. Facts are certain, and they are true. Elementary, you say? Maybe the definition is simple but applying it has been the subject of philosophers and scientists for centuries. We'll talk more about facts later, but for now let's just say that it is something that we know to be true, whether it is because we observed a certain action, scientists tested a physical principle in a lab, historians have used rigorous methods to ascertain its existence, etc. Facts are the bricks that make up critical thought.

Logic is the mortar binding the facts together. We will also talk logic more in-depth later on in the book, but for now, logic is simply the set of rules and relationships governing claims about the truth and falsity of statements. In plain English, logic lets us determine when we can say two different statements lead to a new statement. The classic example in freshman philosophy classes is "All men are mortal. Socrates is a man. Therefore, Socrates is a mortal man." It sounds basic both since all of us have already internalized some level of logical thinking, and because this common sense statement disguises an abstract law of logic. In this argument, the premises, or the starting points established as true for the sake of discussion, do allow us to make a new statement. We also know that we cannot say "All mortals are men" because our experience shows that there are mortals who are not men.

In this case, logic doesn't allow us to make the statement "All mortals are men." It does not follow from the premises, and it creates an invalid relationship according to other rules of logic. Logic prevents us from making contradictory statements, from saying things that simply do not make literal sense.

A defendant's alibi is a simple example of logic preventing invalid conclusions. If we know that the accused was in a different place during the actual crime, we dismiss the case because we also know that a person cannot be in two places at the same time. It's also why we tend to be suspicious of politicians who make contradictory claims—you can either want to do something when you're in the office or not want to do it. Saying two different things is not only confusing when it comes to predicting the candidate's policies, but it is also logically invalid. We won't be reviewing the rather large topic formal symbolic language in this book, but we will rely on logical relationships.

Logic lets us gather facts into new insights, rather than letting facts simply exist like so many pieces of a broken puzzle. Conversely, facts make logic have real consequences, rather than simply remaining abstract figures on paper. Facts and logic are the foundation for critical thinking, so get into the habit of identifying the facts and logic behind the statements and attitudes around you, including your own. You may find considerable gaps in this area, allowing you to question things and present new ideas, or you might be able to reinforce those statements with facts and logic. The point is that in critical thinking, supporting our statements is as important as making them in the first place, and there are specific ways we should be supporting those statements.

Intellectual Rigor

Just like there are certain standards that determine if food is safe or a ball has been thrown out of bounds, critical thinking asserts that there are standards when it comes to how we justify our thoughts and claims.

US Senator Daniel Moynihan once famously stated that "Everyone is entitled to his own opinion, but not his own facts." This is a classic statement of critical thinking. We'll talk more about facts later, but for now let's just say that a fact is a statement that has "truth value," meaning It can either be true or false. An opinion is a subjective matter. We may feel strongly about it, but it is not true or false in any sense beyond the opinion holder's mind or heart. When we assert something as factual, we are inherently making a claim about its truth value and why we are asserting it is true or false. Confusing fact and opinion is a symptom of muddled thinking, and critical thinking tries to remove that confusion.

How we arrive at the particular truth value of a certain statement should conform to standards of clear thinking, evidence, and rationality. Let's say somebody made the statement "All red-haired people are stupid." You could take that statement at face value, but that wouldn't be an example of critical thinking on your part. You could try to interview every single redhead around the world, but even if you could do that, you'd likely soon meet an intelligent redhead that disproved the speaker's statement. So, how might that person justify that statement? They might say they have met a lot of redheads and found them to be stupid. Yet again, a lot of redheads is not the same thing as all red-heads. Also, how did this person establish their stupidity? Do they have an intelligence test? Was that test designed by people with valid measures of intelligence? There was likely no such test. Like all statements of prejudice against a group, this statement will eventually have to fall back on a subjective value judgment that has no truth value—for example, an opinion being used to support a false statement.

The intellectual rigor of critical thinking can often seem harsh or insulting. After all, anytime that standards are asserted, there will be varying levels of different people meeting or falling short of those standards. "How could you vote for that person?" is a well-known inquiry that can expose a lack of critical thinking on the voter's part and even a sense of smugness from the one asking the question. Voters don't always vote rationally, according to the facts, or even according to their own self-interest in the long term. They often rely on first impressions, catchy slogans, and rhetoric, or the opinions of those around them. Critical thinking may not always put the best person in the office, but it will be the best method to make that determination. Awareness of flawed thinking is painful, but it is necessary if we care about critical thought informing important choices.

Intellectual rigor can seem like the most daunting aspect of critical thinking, but it is also most rewarding. It takes effort, concentration, time, and probably some reading and studying when we're especially hard-pressed for an explanation. Yet we are also challenging those around us, and ourselves, to rise to a higher standard.

Seeking Straight Answers

Another large part of critical thinking is the ability to explain why you are doing something with a careful, reasoned explanation (rather than simply saying "Because I felt like it" or "Someone told me to do it"). While this may sound rather lofty, at the same time your explanation should be clear and orderly. It should reflect a clear line of thought, traceable back to factual premises, and it sticks to the facts as well as the topic at hand. Irrelevant information, ideas that don't flow, or off-topic tangents are another sign of a poor argument.

Have you ever encountered someone who replied to a question without actually answering it? Did they get off-topic or immediately shift to a whole new topic? Critical thinking ensures you stay on-point. Steering the person back to the question not only demonstrates a sharp mind but simply gets you an answer to your question.

Did the person answer your question with a lot of jargon—for example, technical terms only known by experts, with vague terms or cliché or without a clear beginning or end to their answer? In other words, did they provide deliberately sloppy or confusing answers? Ask them to make their answer clearer, sticking to simple terms. Critical thinking is not (always) a matter of complex language, fancy terms, or long-winded responses. Clarity of thought and communication is a hallmark of critical thinking.

Thinking About Your Thoughts

Without sounding too abstract, critical thinking involves thinking about our thinking. In plain English, it means paying attention to how we derive judgment. It entails holding our decisions to a higher standard.

The simple act of asking ourselves "why" we do certain things or even have certain opinions or attitudes is a huge part of critical thinking. Many organizations have powerful mission statements, which outline the organization's purpose and philosophy so that management and staff alike can always remind themselves why they work there in the first place. On the ground level, projects often get off-track because the project goals are no longer the focus. Sometimes simply asking Why certain things are being done again can help people focus back on the goals.

The "Why" question can often lead to "how," generating broad questions that can actually lead to specific understanding. "How did I come to believe in the things I now believe?" may sound like an unnecessarily abstract--and possibly intimidating--question, but it could also lead to a better understanding of ourselves and our values. Instead of answering, "that's just what I believe," you begin to have concrete, articulate explanations for your beliefs.

Above all, critical thinking concerns itself with the method—with how we arrive at a judgment. It's why a scientific experiment operates according to accepted practices based upon scientific data: so that the experimenter can say that his results are based upon an established method, not mere conjecture or sloppy design that might have thrown off the results. It's also why we have standards when it comes to things like construction or food safety. The method leading up to the result must itself be sound, or we cannot rely on that result.

In your own life, simply asking "What was my chain of thought leading up to this decision or judgment?" is a crucial act of critical thought. You may discover you didn't have all of the information needed when you made a choice—or that some of your attitudes are more the result of a particular upbringing and hearing the same ideas.

Rather than being something passive we do between action, thought becomes an active guide to those actions, something we are aware of and can therefore subject to scrutiny, in order to improve it.

You're The One in Charge

Critical thinking is the discipline of taking full responsibility for your thoughts and deeds. You are the one who arrives at a conclusion based upon evidence examined by you, actual experiences you've had, and logically approaching the world around you. Your beliefs are your own, rather than ideas forced upon you by habit, circumstance, threats, or other external factors. You are taking charge of the ideas and stimuli around you and subjecting them to examination. You may incorporate other people's ideas, but only when the ideas themselves have been vetted--not because the person giving you those ideas claims to know more, not even if everyone else tells you that they know more.

There is any number of political debates about a slew of topics going on at any time in this country. Just flip on the television or check a social media website, and you can hear someone citing statistics to back up their side in the debate. Next time that happens, try conducting your own research. Check where the speaker may have found their data. Did the speaker leave anything out? If you can find the source, look into whether that source has any political or economic interest in a particular political outcome for that issue. Then find out if another source has a different set of statistics or even a different interpretation of those numbers. Contrary to popular belief, even though "numbers don't lie," they can be conveniently abbreviated or interpreted to suit one side's needs.

You may find two different interpretations of the statistics, or even two completely different statistics. You may then need to determine which of the two is more reliable according to a neutral source, or if anyone is actually presenting the whole picture. The point of this exercise isn't for you to establish rock-bottom certainty on an issue (though if you can, good for you). The purpose is to familiarize yourself with not accepting everything at face value, with questioning claims around you and with using your own mind to find out more and draw your own conclusions. That is critical thinking in a nutshell

The German philosopher Immanuel Kant famously advised people "Dare to know!" This perhaps odd little phrase carries with it a rather subtle definition of "knowing." For Kant, his fellow Enlightenment thinkers, and critical thinkers throughout history, "knowing" is a deeply personal, self-determined act. Kant was reacting against a culture built around following a certain authority without question. At a time when more voices than ever claim authority, his advice is timely as ever.

Brainstorming for Critical Thinking

This is the method where people use brains to storm or examine a problem. Its aim is to develop many ideas in the shortest possible time to solve an identified problem. The generated ideas eventually help to find the best solution possible for a given problem.

How Is Brainstorming Applied

Brainstorming is a tool applied in many institutions so as to generate as many ideas as possible in a team. The focus is usually on the number of ideas brought up but not the quality of the ideas. The groups are usually made up of 5 to 15 people with attention put into the composition of the group. A consideration is made to ensure there is a variety of experience, knowledge, and backgrounds in order to produce varied ideas from varied perspectives.

Brainstorming is usually applied at the beginning of a project when there is no clear definition of the project possibilities. This is a useful way of coming up with ideas that are creative in production methods or product development. Marketing and advertising objects are popular for brainstorming. Brainstorming helps stimulate a group's creativity and encourages the bringing up of unconventional ideas. Every contribution is welcome and may lead to a diversity of ideas.

It is imperative for there to be a clearly defined question before brainstorming starts. However, it is important to note that brainstorming is not as effective on problems that are complex or difficult to describe or those that require specialized knowledge.

Rules of Brainstorming

The most important rule is 'postponement of judgment.' Criticism or feedback is not allowed during the brainstorming session. Every idea is welcome whether common or uncommon, obvious to absurd, impossible to clever ideas. Brainstorming is about gathering as many ideas as possible when criticism is introduced, it blocks free thinking and discourages contribution of ideas instead of motivating each other to generate more ideas. In a brainstorming session, every person must feel free and safe to contribute. The rules in brainstorming are to allow space and remove any obstacles to allow free thinking. Some of these rules are:

1. Postpone judgment – every idea is good, acceptable and noted down, criticism waits for later
2. Focus on quantity – the aim is to gather as many ideas as possible
3. Freewheel – there is freedom to jump from one idea to the next and even to think aloud
4. Hitchhike – it is allowed to hitchhike on another idea and apply synergy and complementing each other by continuing to work on the idea

The Process of Brainstorming

Brainstorming usually takes place in a session, where participants gather together to stimulate and motivate each other to come up with many ideas. The session begins with a well-defined and stated problem. This enables everyone to be able to focus on ideas that are aimed at answering the question or solving the problem. In a brainstorm session, there is usually the team leader who directs the discussion. There are various phases of brainstorming. These are:

1. *Preparation*

   The sessions comprise of about 5 to 15 laymen and experts. The group is informed beforehand the problem or question to be discussed, date, time and duration of the brainstorming session. All the materials needed are prepared by the team leader prior to the session.

2. *Generate Ideas*

   All ideas that are generated are noted down on a flip chart or sticky notes or even recorded by the team leader. The team leader ensures every person participates and gives their ideas and creates a relaxed and creative atmosphere. This first phase of generating ideas is called the divergence phase because of the diverse ideas generated. The next phase is the convergence phase where the different ideas are grouped together into related subjects.

3. *Evaluation*

After the brainstorming session is over, an evaluation of all ideas is done. This part can be done using the same participants or narrowing the group further down. Evaluate the usefulness of the ideas on each topic of discussion, analyze their pros and cons and compare the ideas to each other. Prioritizing takes place, and the hanging fruits or ideas that offer immediate possible solutions are given first priority. When you filter the best and most useful ideas, you begin to move from quantity to quality.

4. *Creativity*

Brainstorming is much more than just presenting ideas, but it is a way of developing more creative ideas in a short time. Every person is creative and is cable of advancing their creative skills. There are several ways to stimulate creativity according to psychology—hence helping you to have better critical thinking skills. These methods include:

- Remember ideas – always ensure you have a pen and paper. Ideas come at any time, and the best way is to note them down immediately to enable you to remember them later by referring to them.
- Challenge yourself – try to do something outside your comfort zone to stimulate new ideas. A new

challenge stimulates the brain to get creative solutions that may also have a positive effect in other areas.

- Widen knowledge and skills – applying knowledge and skills to new situations is called creativity. Learn new skills by attending seminars, reading or watching documentaries. Stay open to learning new things—hence stimulating your brain to be more creative in thinking.
- Stimuli – creativity is promoted in an environment with stimuli like music. Stimuli provide impulses for the brain to be more creative in thinking.

Bloom's Taxonomy and Critical Thinking

This is a known classification of learning. Educators use the guidelines in Bloom's taxonomy to develop a method to incorporate critical thinking into their pupils' education. Application and analysis are higher order skills usually associated with upper-division curriculum while knowledge and comprehension that are said to be lower order thinking skills are offered through basic courses.

Bloom's Lower Order Thinking Skills

According to Bloom, the lower order thinking skills are those of knowledge, application, and comprehension. They indicate how a pupil is able to recite information, dates, facts and solve problems by organizing the information and applying basic concepts to arrive at solutions. Some of the keywords found here will include:

- Develop
- Utilize
- Demonstrate
- Explain
- Recall
- Build
- Choose
- Define
- Find

When defining the objectives of learning in lower-division courses, these keywords are used.

Bloom's Higher Order Thinking Skills

These refer to the need synthesis, analysis, and evaluation. A person showing this level of cognitive skills will group details—trying to come up with a choice through both comparing as well as contrasting. Some of the characteristics of higher order thinking skills include:

- Developing
- Evaluating
- Justifying

- Measuring
- Designing
- Combining
- Creating

A pupil from the upper-division course is expected to have the ability to exhibit every skill if faced with tough problems.

Critical Thinking According to Bloom

Critical thinking abilities are important in both the lower and higher order thinking according to Bloom. He describes critical thinking as comprising two elements:

1. Skills for generating details (lower order)
2. Utilizing them in directing actions (higher order)

To analytically think through given details to make cognizant choices necessitates a thinker to navigate through the six levels in cognitive thinking according to Bloom. These levels are:

- Knowledge
- Comprehension
- Application
- Analysis
- Synthesis
- Evaluation

He further says that major decisions done haphazardly are likely to produce unsatisfactory results.

The best method to avoid this is through asking questions, which will show that a student is using lower order thinking to solve problems use or begin with the keywords like "who," "why," "when," and "what." These kinds of questions begin with those at a lower degree. Meanwhile, the higher order level ones may come like, *"How can you?" or "What evidence have you found?"* Other questions of thinking at a higher level may come designed as *"Do you support something?"* or *"How would you classify?"* These kinds of questions usually help a student evaluate and analyze information so as to make informed decisions that will give satisfactory results.

Even as much as there is evidence to support the importance of critical thinking, there are misconceptions that are universal and must be addressed.

1. Critical thinking has been viewed as something design to eradicate ideas. This is nothing but misconception, as what critical thinking does is to bring ideas into perspective.
2. Critical thinking leads to overthinking and slow decision-making or total incapability of making decisions due to fixating over something pointless. However, this is

another misconception because the aim of critical thinking is to ensure cognizant choices.

3. One more misunderstanding is that it makes a thinker cold and unfeeling, which is false, as the overall process is rooted in doubting and questioning even oneself.

As soon as a person has been able to overcome or gets past the misconceptions, he or she can climb the Bloom's levels of critical thinking and thus achieve the goal.

Aspects of Critical Thinking

Solutions to certain problems need to be arrived at instantaneously putting in mind that problems never provide time to be ready and accept them. Anyone can arrive at optimal solutions to a problem if given time, but some problems need a solution immediately. With these, people tend to make very quick decisions. Studies have shown that decisions that are made in a hurry most often are found to be wrong and take a lot of time and resources to correct them. It has been established that when people are faced with quick decision-making, they are likely to leave out some of the important parameters that need to be considered and are significant in the solution of the particular problem.

Creative thinking is not an art that can be adopted and trained, but it develops out of practice. To be a creative thinker, you must think in different angles with respect to different situations and considering the problem from different perspectives. This will help in arriving at a comprehensive, optimal and quantitative solution.

Based on problem-solving approaches, certain aspects of critical thinking are established:

- Quick thinking – this is a trait that enables a person to give accurate answers to sudden questions or situations. Quick thinkers take relatively shorter periods at a time to arrive at solutions as compared to general thinkers. Quick thinking is a skill developed over a period of time and requires patience, but with practice, this skill is attainable.
- Creative thinking – sometimes, people may stop reacting to a certain situation or problem. They wrongly assume that the problem aroused is a new situation that they are unfamiliar with and so they ignore it and proceed to accomplish other tasks that they feel capable of handling. This will definitely hamper their analytical and creative skills that are essential in developing creative thinking.
- Analytical thinking – through analytical thinking, a person is able to define and determine a problem and come up with the best solution amongst many possible solutions.

How to Develop Critical Thinking Skills

How do you react to situations? Do you react according to your emotions or based on your personal biases? Do you ever find yourself in need of improving your communication with the people around you? Critical thinking skills are able to help you enhance your ability to make objective and effective arguments. Lack of these skills will make arguments seem to be one side— criticism can often fell like a personal attack instead of an opportunity to openly and productively communicate.

How then do you develop these critical thinking skills that will help you navigate through any situation while setting aside emotions and making decisions that are insightful? Below are some strategies that will help you in developing critical thinking skills:

1. Be self-critical – becoming your own critic for your thoughts and actions is the first step to acquiring these skills. Self-reflection is the key to personal growth. Break down your thoughts by questioning why you believe something. After doing this, objectively assess this information and establish solid logic of your beliefs. Instead of just an idea, ask questions like, *"What makes me believe this? Is there any time in my life this proved to be false or true? Am I emotionally attached to this idea? If so, why?"* Self-reflection is important because it enables you to see how you respond to a situation in your mind and out loud.

Acknowledging your strengths and weaknesses, personal preferences, and biases is another way of becoming a self-critic. Having this information enables you to understand why you approach different situations in certain ways and step around that viewpoint because you are aware of it.

2. Active listening – it is almost impossible to think and listen at the same time. To become a critical thinker, you must be able to listen to other people's arguments, ideas and criticisms without thinking of how you are going to respond or reaction while they are speaking. Without truly listening, you cannot be able to absorb the information someone is giving to you. When you listen you develop empathy. Hearing the other person's perspective enables you to pick that information and analyze it because we fully understand it and come up with the best possible answer or solution.

3. Analyzing information – analyzing of information is very central to critical thinking. A lot of times, we struggle to focus on the issue at hand either because of our emotions or other factors. To successfully find a solution, we need to analyze the information we have. We need to carefully assess what is being said and understand what is expected or needed. After this, it is possible to analyze all arguments even our own arguments and evaluate how the decisions will affect others. Stepping back to analyze an

argument gives way to objectivity which is crucial in finding solutions or problem-solving.

4. Nonviolent communication – critical thinking will not help if you are unable to communicate in a productive nonviolent way. You must have the ability to recognize logic when you listen and analyze different situations. Be able to communicate in a productive nonviolent way with compassion, collaboration, and observation. When you approach a given situation with compassion, your mindset is that of peace instead of a defensive one. This will enable you to observe your arguments as well of others without bias and judgment. Emotions are detached, and collaboration happens when everyone comes with compassion and an open mind.

5. Developing a foresight – foresight is the ability to foresee or predict the future impact of a decision. Foresight is an important aspect of success in your life. For instance, if you are moving the location of your business, you need to analyze the impact of your decision. Will it be too far? Are you likely to lose business because of the change? What are the advantages of the move? You should be able to weigh each decision carefully before you completely settle on it.

Critical thinking needs the ability to assess your own beliefs as well as other people's ideas. It is the ability to listen actively, dissect, assess and rate arguments and separation of emotions from the matter at hand.

Critical Thinking and Problem Solving

Many people believe that your feelings are separate or independent of your thoughts, but the truth is that feelings are as a result of your thoughts. This revelation is very enlightening as well as liberating. It is enlightening because you realize that we are responsible for our attitudes because the power to decide our perspective, our thoughts, and our mood is in our hands.

When you are aware that you can choose and decide your thinking, you discover that you have the ability to best control the circumstances in your life, enhance your decision-making abilities and live a life that is more productive.

We think critically with a mindset of problem-solving when we:

- Depend on reason and not emotions
- Analyze a wide range of viewpoints and perspectives
- Have an open mind to other interpretations
- Acknowledge new evidence, explanations, and results
- Are always willing to re-evaluate information
- Can separate from personal biases and prejudices
- Be considerate of all possibilities

- Avoid forming quick conclusions

Just like all other skills, developing knowledge in critical thinking or problem-solving takes time, practice, and perseverance.

Step-by-Step Critical Thinking for Problem Solving

1. Identify the problem – first identify if there exists a problem to be solved. It is possible that after thinking this through you realize there is no problem but a misunderstanding. If then there is a problem, you need to identify the exact problem. Try and analyze the pros and cons of the problem, define and state it.

2. Analyze the problem – after identifying the problem, now analyze it using different perspectives and ask questions like is it possible to solve it? Do you need help to solve it? The advantage of looking at a problem in different angles is that you may be able to come up with a solution immediately. You may also be able to identify a narrow point of view or bias that needs to be expanded.

3. Brainstorm – brainstorming is important as it enables you to come up with several possible solutions. Put down any possible solution, go through the list once again and narrow it down until you arrive at the best possible solution. When you come up with several possible

solutions, makes it easier for you to find the ultimate solution.

4. Decide on the best solution – go through your list of proposed solutions. Take your time and determine what solution amongst the ones you have best suits the situation.

5. Take action – now it is time to implement your solution. Every problem has a solution. Do practice approaching problems as opportunities and not as obstacles. This will help you enhance your problem-solving and critical thinking skills.

For every problem that you are able to solve, it increases your self-worth and confidence. Critical thinking enables you to handle future problems with more skill and increases your experience as you gain perspective.

Phases of Critical Thinking

Critical thinking has also been defined as the process of learning to think better by improving one's thinking skills. Critical thinkers use the process to evaluate, synthesize what was learned or currently being learned, and then find solutions to problems. Unfortunately, most people's thinking is biased, unclear, imprecise, uninformed or prejudiced. For this reason, critical thinking is needed to improve this aspect.

In an organization, critical thinking is necessary to overcome problems, make modifications or changes in the work structures and culture. Developing critical thinking skills is gradual. It involves learning and maintaining a serious focus on the process and transforming personal habits in thought and long development time.

Critical thinking is not about saying something that is not well thought through, guessing on solutions, memorizing on materials to evaluate, believing something because everyone else believes the same or arguing about something without facts.

Qualities of a Critical Thinker

- Deep thinkers
- Self-disciplined
- Self-monitored
- Self-directed
- Self-corrective.

Critical thinkers usually question or raise problems, and they proceed to come up with the best appropriate solutions to them. They collect, gather and analyze relevant information in order to find a solution to a certain situation as they test them against relevant standards – logic. They also keep their minds open to other alternative systems of thought as they continue to recognize and assess their assumptions and basis of their reasoning. Critical thinkers are also effective communicators with others for the purposes of finding solutions to problems.

There are six different developmental phases of critical thinking that lead to the mastering of the skills in critical thinking. With a lot of practice and use of the process, an individual can begin transforming their thought habits and embrace critical thinking skills. These phases are:

Phase 1: The Unenlightened Thinker

Here, a person is not consciously aware that there exists a problem within their thinking patterns

Phase 2: The Confronted Thinker

The individual is aware that there are problems in their thinking process

Phase 3: The Novice Thinker

Here, an individual will try to improve their thinking but not making it a consistent practice.

Phase 4: Proactive Thinker

They recognize it is important to practice critical thinking in order to improve

Phase 5: Developed Thinker

Here, an individual starts growth in critical thinking based on their regular practice

Phase 6: The Mastery Thinker

Here an individual is more skilled and aware. Evaluative, reflective and analytical thinking become part of him.

The development of critical thinking comes through these phases once a person acknowledges that there are flaws in their way of thinking. They must accept to be challenged in the process and make a point to practice more and more.

The Framework of Critical Thinking

As earlier discussed, there are many definitions of critical thinking but all based on a similar concept. In this case, we define critical thinking as that type of thinking about any problem, subject or content where the thinker improves their quality of thinking by skillfully being in charge of all the structures necessary in thinking and infusing intellectual standards on them. According to Paul and Elder, the critical thinking framework has 3 components:

- The elements of thought or reasoning;
- The intellectual standards that are applied to the reasoning; and

- The intellectual traits, which come from consistent and disciplined use of intellectual standards in thinking.

Elements of Thought/Reasoning

The components or elements of thinking are:

- There is a purpose in every reasoning.
- The reasoning is for the purposes of finding out something, answering questions, and solving problems.
- Every reasoning is based upon assumptions
- Every reasoning comes from some point of view
- Every reasoning is based on information, evidence, and data
- Every reasoning is shaped and expressed through ideas and concepts
- Every reasoning has inferences or interpretations that influence outcomes and give meaning to data.
- Every reasoning has consequences and implications.

Universal Intellectual Standards

These are the elements used in determining the quality of reasoning. Critical thinking requires one to have a good command of these standards. The purpose of this is to ensure that the standards of reasoning are completely infused in thinking and become a guide to improved reasoning. These standards include:

- Clarity
  - Can you demonstrate what you mean?
  - Can you give examples?
  - Can you offer more information?

- Accuracy
  - How can we confirm that?
  - How is it true?
  - How do we test and verify that?

- Precision
  - Can you provide more details?
  - Can you be more specific?
  - Can you be more exact?

- Relevance
  - What is its relationship to the problem?
  - How does it bear to the question?
  - Of what help is it to the issue?

- Depth
  - Which factors make it difficult?
  - What complexities do you find in this question?
  - What challenges do we need to deal with?

- Breadth

- Is there another perspective to look at this?
- Should we consider a different viewpoint?
- Do we need to view this in other ways?

- Logic
  - Does it all make sense when put together?
  - Do your paragraphs fit in together?
  - Does what you say go according to the evidence provided?

- Significance
  - Is this the most crucial challenge or problem?
  - Is this the idea we should focus on?
  - Which facts are most important among these?

- Fairness
  - Can your thinking be justified based on context?
  - Am I considering the thinking of others?
  - Is my goal fair based on the situation?
  - Are you using concepts based on educated usage or are you distorting them to get what you want?

Intellectual Traits

When you consistently apply standards of thinking to elements of thinking, it results in developing the following intellectual traits:

- Intellectual courage
- Fair-mindedness
- Intellectual perseverance
- Intellectual humility
- Intellectual autonomy
- Intellectual empathy
- Confidence in reasoning
- Intellectual integrity

Characteristics of a Critical Thinker

Regular using of the intellectual traits usually results in a cultivated critical thinker that is able to do the following:

- Identify important questions and problems, articulating them very clearly and precisely
- Collect and evaluate useful information with the use of abstract ideas in order to accurately and effectively interpret it.
- Come to well-thought conclusions and testing them against set standards and relevant criteria
- Be open-minded in reasoning within different systems of thought, understanding and evaluating as needed, their assumptions, practical consequences, and implications
- Effectively communicate to figure out solutions to problems with others.

Critical thinking is both an art and science in nature. It is a concept that needs to be developed and worked on daily. This concept allows the thinker to be in charge of his/her thoughts and to be completely objective and understanding of their personal biases in problem-solving and decision-making. Critical thinking skills are important in every aspect of life and make facing life's challenges much easier as you have a sure process of solving them to find the best conclusions.

CHAPTER TWO: BENEFITS OF CRITICAL THINKING

Critical thinking does involve a fair amount of thought, energy, and time (though it involves less and less the more you do it). So why would you do it? After all, lots of people go through life-changing decisions based upon incomplete information, judging things according to unexamined assumptions, or simply doing what everyone says they should do without ever asking why.

Putting aside value judgment about how anyone should live their lives, the following are a few practical benefits to incorporating critical thinking into your life:

- You'll Achieve the Best for You

  While certain academic disciplines and professions are popularly associated with critical thinking, it actually transcends any one subject or function. Critical thinking represents a deeper examination of things, understanding problems, situations, questions, and even people on a much more substantive level. It can be applied in a number of areas in your own life—allowing you to analyze and evaluate an important decision or a lengthy project according to the facts and move forward with confidence.

- You'll Anticipate (Most of) The Unexpected

"Measure two times; cut a single time" is an old proverb reminding us that even a little extra time at the start of a project can help avoid mistakes later on, while hasty actions can result in unforeseen negative consequences. Critical thinking, taking the time to analyze the facts, evaluate the information, and develop a plan according to those considerations may not anticipate all problems but will help you see what might happen and be ready for the unexpected.

- You'll Stay One Step Ahead

George C. Parker was the man who infamously pretended to sell the Brooklyn Bridge to unsuspecting, naive folks. Parker did eventually go to jail for fraud, but in the meantime, a lot of people lost their hard-earned money—and perhaps their dignity. While not every con is on this level, unfortunately, we do live in a world filled with people and organizations attempting to manipulate us into giving away our money, our personal support, and anything else they want to get ahold of. If something sounds too good to be true, critical thinking lets you examine things to find out if it's at all true.

- You'll Sharpen Your Mind

Just like you may exercise in the gym to get into physical shape, critical thinking is a great way to get your mind into shape. Critical thinking challenges you to look deep into things, to not accept easy answers or superficial explanations, and to think hard about the world around you.

- You'll Improve Your Performance

Professional development courses, executive training, and other programs aimed at improving productivity all teach some form of critical thinking. They may use different terms or apply it to different situations, but they all rely upon self-awareness, clear thinking, and rational analysis as tools to "get ahead" in the workplace. Regardless of your job, critical thinking can make your work easier and increase productivity, which are good things for both you and your boss!

- You'll Understand More

While critical thinking can be time-consuming and often requires concentration, the more you do it, the more naturally it will come to you, and the more you will find yourself applying it out of habit. Day-to-day chores begin to seem like opportunities for imaginative problem-solving. The conversation becomes deeper and more interesting, as you not only hear what people have to say but consider how they may have come to a certain conclusion or developed a particular outlook. Looking at the world with a critical eye does not mean finding fault with everything around you. It means looking at familiar attitudes and experiences in a fresh light.

Importance of Critical Thinking

The ability to analyze your thoughts and present them with evidence instead of accepting your personal ideas without sufficient proof is what is called critical thinking. There are many benefits to critical thinking as well as the importance of critical thinking. Critical thinking skills are used in the classrooms to solve problems as well as being used in real-world situations. It is a valuable skill to master by both students and employees.

There are a variety of skills that you can learn through critical thinking skills that you can apply anywhere necessitating reflection, planning, as well as analysis. A domain skill is that skill you need in every aspect of your life. Critical thinking skills are needed in every area of life. Regardless of where you work whether in education, research, legal profession, management and so forth, you need critical thinking skills. The ability to reason out factually as well as systematically provide solutions is a great advantage in whatever industry you are in. There are many areas where critical thinking skills are applied and play an important role. These will include:

- Economy

  In the new knowledge economy, critical thinking is very important. Information and technology are what drives the global economy. One must be in a position to deal with changes effectively and speedily. There is an increased demand for people who are not only fixated to one aspect of intellect. The capability of critically thinking as well as analyzing information and incorporating different sources of knowledge to solve problems is an added advantage. Good critical reasoning promotes this kind of abilities, making it extremely vital nowadays.

- Language and presentation skills

  Critical thinking improves your presentation skills and language. Systematic and clear thinking improves the way you express your thoughts. Through understanding the ways of evaluating the logic behind any text, your comprehension improves significantly.

- Promotes creativity

  Coming up with an inventive solution to a problem is usually more than just an idea. The new ideas must be relevant to the task at hand; hence, critical thinking is very crucial in evaluating new ideas, deciding on the best ones, and adjusting them where necessary.

- Self-reflection

  Self-reflection is very important in order to live a meaningful life. Critical thinking helps a person in self-reflection by providing the tools necessary for self-evaluation.

- Foundation of science and a democratic society

  In order to experiment and confirm theories, scientists require critical thinking skills, as these are what fundamentally compose the modern, technological, progressive civilization we are in—which is essentially dependent on the general populace's ability and willingness to critically perceive reality and offer their judgment with the general good in mind.

- Academic performance

  For a student, learning critical thinking skills is very important because they enhance your performance. Studies have shown that students that are able to critique and analyze information also suggest the intersectionality with the various social phenomena that we experience daily through applying these in their daily lives as they understand the content at a deeper-lasting level.

  Instead of depending on teachers and classroom for instructions, students that have critical thinking skills are independent and self-directed learners. They are also able to evaluate the way they learn, examine the areas where they're strong and weak, and lead the path they wish to take in school.

Traits of a Good Critical Thinker

- A good critical thinker is able to separate facts from opinions, to analyze an issue from both sides and to make rational inferences and withhold personal biases or judgment.

- They usually calm people down where there is mass hysteria or panic. They are able to skillfully contemplate on every single one of the alternatives then eventually provide the best solution they can muster.

- Critical thinkers are generally calm and know when they are correct. They're unlikely to be fooled, as it is second nature to them to question everything and base their decisions on established facts. They are not like others who do not question the source of the information they receive.

- They must take into account every single choice prior to making a concrete move. For instance, should a decision needs to be made almost immediately, it is second nature to them to look at the most time-efficient way to achieve the goal they set out for. Critical thinkers put a lot of emphasis on efficiency.

- A critical thinker is self-aware. This means that they are able to know which is an outcome of logic and which is of emotion or impulse. When able to understand your personal perspective, you are well able to consider the perspectives of others and then be able to form informed conclusions based on facts, not feelings.

Benefits of Critical Thinking in the Workplace

Critical thinking in the workplace is very important. It forces employees and employers or managers to look at situations and come up with all possible solutions may be through brainstorming before settling on an answer. Any business, regardless if it is small or big, will benefit from critical thinking. Some of the benefits of critical thinking in the workplace are:

Brings New Ideas

A common reaction when an issue arises in the workplace is that it falls in a predetermined category. In critical thinking, this kind of assumption does not happen. Using the skills of critical thinking in the workplace eliminates the temptation to categorize every issue under something that happened before. Managers and employees are forced to look over conventional solutions and come up with new ideas that efficiently address the problem if they apply critical thinking skills—hence bringing in new ideas.

Fosters Teamwork

Every person in the entire workforce can get involved in solving problems through the application of the critical thinking process. This is where brainstorming comes in in an organization. When more people are involved, more solutions or ideas are presented. In the workplace, there are people from diverse backgrounds, and they can come together each giving their own idea based on their understanding, experience, and expertise. This fosters teamwork as different employees come together to find a solution through working together. Employees feel appreciated and feel that they have been given a chance to impact the future of the organization. Critical thinking promotes tolerance in the workplace and understanding.

Promotes Options

The advantage of critical thinking in the workplace is that the company is able to develop many viable solutions to the same problem. This promotes workplace innovation as well as being able to offer varied solutions to clients. Having several solutions to a problem in a company allows your company to use available resources instead of purchasing new materials. This will save money for your company, and customers will benefit from having a variety of solutions to choose from.

Uncovering Spinoffs

Deeply thinking into ways of solving an issue can bring information that can be applied to other areas. For instance, a critical thinking exercise on handling a manufacturing process may lead to other ideas of different manufacturing methods. When you begin asking critical questions about one idea, it can lead you to solutions of other unsolved challenges.

Critical Thinking in Day-to-Day Life

It's not merely an idea but rather something that exists in the real world and applicable to not only your workplace but also to the various facets of your daily life as well. It is the technique that necessitates to logically think prior to deciding on something and is capable of revolutionizing various aspects of the reality in which you exist through your thought process, problem-solving skills, as well as rationalizations. Oftentimes, critical thinking has been misjudged as criticism, but instead, it is a system that follows logical steps to arrive at an appropriate conclusion. There are several ways that critical thinking can help you in your day-to-day life. Some of these are:

1) Approach – critical thinking makes you aware of different approaches to a problem and the ability to critically analyze those approaches. With these skills, you will not rely on a blanket problem-solving method, but you learn

how to recognize other approaches that can be more valuable—hence improving your success.

2) Save time – when you think critically, it's already known to you what details are relevant and not to the solving of your problem—hence, you save time. Anchored to this is your ability to know your priorities and make your decisions as time-efficient as possible.

3) An appreciation of differing worldviews – learning how to empathize with other views leads you to appreciate every viewpoint presented. When faced with day-to-day situations, critical thinking helps you not to be judgmental but instead to be tolerant and appreciative of other views.

4) Enhanced communication – by learning how to analyze situations or information, you will find you are better able to communicate with friends and co-workers well and avoid conflicts. In the workplace, it helps you become a better communicator because you base your communication on consistent and factual information, not on heresy or assumptions.

5) Decision-Making – your decision-making abilities are transformed with critical thinking and are made much easier. You don't make decisions on guesswork, but you work on a more considered and analytical basis that result in sound decisions.

6) Reason – with critical thinking skills, the way you solve any problem improves. Basing your decisions on logic and facts rather than emotions or instinct makes for a sound problem-solving technique.

Most of the times we tend to think on our feet without giving much attention to our thoughts. Many decisions that we make following this way, we regret them later. It is important always to take a moment and analyze the information presented to you in order to make decisions that you will never regret, considering the benefits of critical thinking that were discussed. Avoid rushed answers or jumping into conclusions but apply critical thinking skills in order to enjoy the benefits of the process as well as making informed decisions.

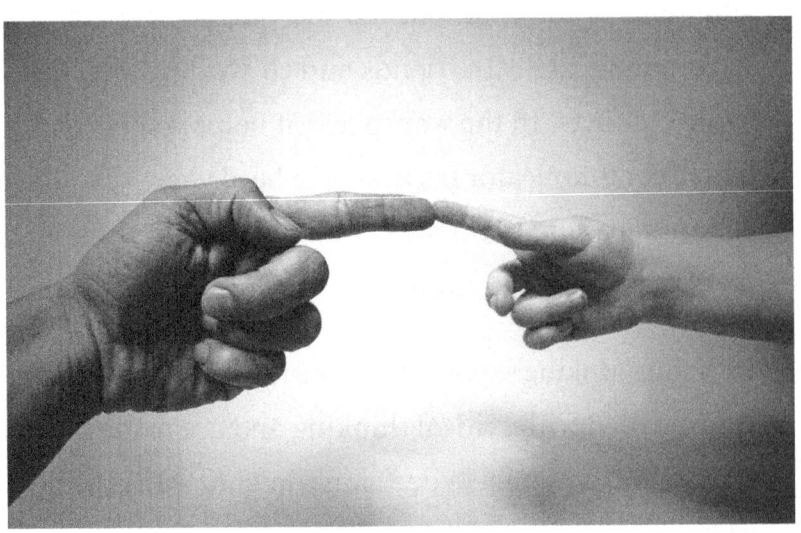

CHAPTER THREE: ROUTINES TO IMPROVE CRITICAL THINKING

This section will introduce some helpful ways to improve your critical thinking. Some of them are more labor-intensive than others, but they all can be done in a fairly short amount of time and don't require any special tools or designated space (though a pen and paper might be useful, depending on your own style).

Take A Breath, and Have a Thought

Begin to take even a moment before you answer a question, decide on a course of action, or make a decision. Train yourself to think carefully—even briefly—about what you are doing and why you are doing it. The world and people around us seem to move faster by the day, but building critical thought into your everyday life can be revealing as well as productive.

Practice Careful Reading and Synthesis of Information

Does your reading ever become a blur? Do you find yourself thinking "Get to the point" when you are in class? Try slowing down, focusing on each sentence, and seeing how all of those separate ideas form a larger point. Treat the comma, periods and other punctuation marks in a sentence as actual stopping points for you to internalize what was just said.

Talk to Yourself

If you find yourself nodding or shaking your head at something said during a conversation or on the news, step back and consider why you made that gesture. What are you agreeing or disagreeing with? Have you always felt that way? When was the last time you thought about the thing you are agreeing or disagreeing with as a topic of consideration—rather than something you simply agree or disagree with?

Break Down a Task into Its Parts

Critical thinking involves understanding a problem at its most basic level, including the different aspects of the issue or task. The next time you have something to do, try breaking it down into the different components that get you to your goal.

It could be as simple as needing to rake leaves:
1. Get the rake out.
2. Collect all the leaves into a pile.
3. Put all the leaves into a bag.

You now have three basic steps to rake the leaves. Is there any way you could rearrange or even shorten the process? For example, what if you combined steps two and three:

1. Get the rake out.
2. Collect all leaves into a bag as you rake them.

This is a very simple example but it shows how even a simple task can be broken down, and perhaps improved on. Could you save time by just keeping the rake out in the yard?

Give Yourself a Real Goal

Do you watch too much television, or do you feel like you actually miss a lot of shows? You can ask the same questions about reading, exercising, or any other daily activity. Critical thinking can help you figure out a means of self-improvement.

First, ask yourself what "enough" or "a lot" looks like. If you watch ten hours of television per week and decide that it is too much, you just defined the terms of your problem. If you then say that you'd like to cut back to six hours of television per week, you just gave yourself a concrete goal—for example, a definite number rather than an abstract one (i.e., "less").

People spend millions of dollars on self-help books. While many of them are helpful and while different things work for different people, a common thread among many of these books is being honest and clear about your goals. Don't just plan to lose weight—plan to lose a certain amount of weight by a certain date. Determining that goal most likely requires input from your doctor or a weight loss professional, qualified people who can help you analyze the right goal. Again, this is just using facts from a trusted source and applying them to your problem using analysis and logic. It's critical thinking.

Know Thy Adversary

As discussed earlier, critical thinking requires objectivity, the ability to separate yourself from emotions and question all assumptions. One good way to practice this skill is to analyze an opposing point of view or even advocate for it. Lawyers do this all the time—a lawyer does not necessarily always represent a person or side they agree with, but their job under the law is to give that side fair representation, which often requires the attorney to argue as though they actually were on that person's side. Lawyers are valued for their critical thinking for precisely this reason—their ability to separate fact from emotion and to make objective claims based strictly on evidence and logic.

Take an opposing viewpoint and consider:

- Why would someone take this side? Remember to be charitable to your opponent—assume, for the sake of this exercise, that they hold their own views for reasons as equally valid as your own, and not because they are ignorant, selfish, etc.

- Consider how this perspective might be beneficial. In your head or on paper, try to argue in favor of it. Can you set aside your own perspective, just for the sake of this exercise?

- Finally, try to argue against your own perspective from the other side. Formulate arguments that the other side may make against your side. This exercise can actually help you to strengthen your own side because you are now anticipating possible objectives as well as weeding out any contradictions or faulty points in your thinking.

The Martian Tourist

Why do you like the things you like? How did you come to like those things over other things? For example, why do you now love certain foods (or dislike others)? When was the first time you tried that food? Was there a pleasant memory associated with it? Have you been eating it for so long you can't even remember actually developing a taste for it? These questions aren't about justifying or explaining your taste in food, art, or other subjective areas, or ascertaining the best piece of music or kind of cuisine. Asking these questions allows you to look at personal preferences from a distance, to understand them and talk about them as something other than parts of you.

As an exercise, say you have a strange alien visitor come to Earth, and ask you to take them to your favorite pastime. Maybe it is watching television, going to a concert, or playing sports. Whatever the activity, this alien has never encountered it before and is not only unfamiliar with its rules or conventions, but it has no idea why any being would find it enjoyable. Try to explain why to them.

What do you enjoy about playing sports? Why would making yourself tired and sweaty be fun? What do the rules of the game add to it, and why are they necessary (as opposed to everyone just doing what they think is fun)? How does the experience of cooperating and competing with other humans add to the enjoyment of this activity?

Best Practices for Improving Critical Thinking Skills

To improve critical thinking skills is a lifelong study that is worth pursuing. Critical thinking is at the center of accumulation of knowledge and experience. After you have begun the practice of critical thinking, the question will be how to keep improving in critical thinking skills. What wisdom can be shared with learners that will help them keep their abilities just as well after their school years?

Teaching critical thinking skills does not require much in planning or equipment but just open and curious open-minds and some strategies like we shall discuss below. These are daily approaches designed to help you through the journey of enhancing and improving critical thinking skills so that they become an unconscious daily practice in a lifetime of learning.

Go through the strategies below carefully, internalize them, and begin to infuse them into your daily practices. Slowly, critical thinking will start becoming second to nature for you.

1. Do not waste time.

We all have had moments where we have wasted time and sadly realize that we cannot recover it back. Time wasted, unfortunately, can never be recovered. It is important to try and minimize the amount of time wasted on trivial things. For instance, instead of sitting in front of a TV set after work flicking through channels, you can spend that time reviewing how and when you practiced thinking throughout the day. Do this by asking yourself questions like these:

- What time did you do your worst thinking?
- When did you do your best thinking?
- What did you think about?
- If you were to repeat the day, what would you do differently?

- Were you able to figure out anything?

You can go through such question and even ask more spending as much time as you possibly can on them by analyzing your responses to the questions. The more practice you put on this, the more you will improve in your thinking patterns and habits.

2. Learn new things every day.

Make learning a lifelong habit. Learn something new every day. What have you always wanted to learn? Go for it. Keep learning until you find the answers that you are searching for regardless of the question you want answers for. Ignore what others may say but focus on gaining knowledge every day. Fulfilling an intellectual need is very important as well as developing curiosity habits to learn more.

It is never too late to learn new things nor is it very late to start new things. Look at history people who started fresh projects an age many people would think it is impossible. If you have ambitions for higher learning, don't get discouraged go for it. Learning has no boundaries—you are free to be curious in any field and learn. Improving critical thinking skills isn't about your age. It is not about conquering the world—it is just learning a new skill that will help you in every aspect of your life. Believe in your potential and learn every day.

3. Have a questioning mind.

Since the beginning of time, the human mind has been curious about everything under the sun and even beyond the sun. In modern times, we encourage and teach our children to question, be curious, and explore possibilities. Questions are the essence of learning.

The ability to ask meaningful questions that will result in useful and constructive answers are at the core of critical thinking and a lifetime of learning. Giving learning through leading questions as the focus ensures that both the learners and the providers do not just accept information presented to them, but they question it and search for different viewpoints because they don't take anything for granted. For instance, think of something that you heard and ask yourself some of the following questions:

- Who said it?
    - Is it someone you know?
    - Is the person in a position of power or authority?
    - Whoever told you this, does it matter?

- What was said?
    - Did they provide opinions or facts?
    - Did they provide all the necessary information?
    - Did they leave out anything?

These questions among many others will help you make an informed decision because you will have applied the critical thinking process.

4. Practice listening actively.

There is this common expression that "many people are waiting for their chance to talk." This means no one is really listening. What do you understand by actively listening when someone is talking? Secondly, how are you able to listen actively to improve your critical thinking skills? Studies have shown that people are inefficient listeners most of the time, that after listening to a presentation that is 10 minutes long, the average listener has understood and retained only 50 percent 48 hours after the presentation and it keeps dropping with the other participants.

Listening is not easy—it is hard work. Active listening requires even more work. Active listening means making conscious and purposeful effort to hear every word being said and most important, understanding the message being delivered. It also is about total comprehension of the speakers' intention—hence having empathy towards the speaker and information being passed. How then do you improve your active listening?

Just like any other communication skill, active listening can be learned, taught, and even practiced. The following tips will help you learn, improve, and practice active listening:

a) Talk Less – it is not possible to talk and listen at the same time. Hold on to responses and interruptions and be open by giving the person speaking the attention and whatever they need by you understanding what they are saying.

b) Adopt a listening mode – silence your environment and mind, open your mind to hear and feel comfortable as you listen. Ensure that you engage in eye contact.

c) Make the speaker feel comfortable – make a nod, utilize your body gestures, or do anything that will make the speaker realize you are listening and interested in what they have to say. Seating is also important for both the speaker and listener. Where is the speaker more comfortable? When you sit behind your desk or sit beside them? If a child, get at their eye level and avoid towering over them it is intimidating to them, and they may not be able to pass the information.

d) Remove distractions – this is about clearing the room of any physical things that may cause distractions, putting your phone on silent, switching off your TV or computer if they were on and may cause distractions. If the speaker requires privacy, ensure you give it to them by asking others in the room to excuse you, and then you close the door. This also gives the speaker the confidence that you will listen and understand all that they will be telling you and your response will be equally good.

e) Empathize – try and understand the situation from where the speaker is coming from. Put yourself in their position, ask necessary questions that will lead you to understand the speaker's position and feeling regarding the situation.

f) Don't fear silence – some people require time to form a response that is thoughtful. Don't rush them, and don't suggest what they should say. This hinders them from communicating honestly. Let them speak at their pace and understanding.

g) Put aside personal prejudice – this is also a very difficult thing to do because our experiences form who we are. To put all these experiences aside is a skill that requires help so as to be able to listen actively.

h) Heed their tone – be keen to understand the tone being used. Sometimes a tone may hide the meaning of a word and other times it may enhance the meaning. Be certain which tone it is so you understand what is being communicated.

i) Listen and identify the underlying meaning - most of the times you realize there is hidden meaning in some communication. Listen to understand or comprehension and secondly for ideas being communicated.

j) Put your attention also to the non-verbal communication – you can miss a lot of information if you are not keen on the non-verbal cues. People can communicate through body language and facial expressions—thus the reason that eye contact is necessary.

5. Solve the problem.

If there are so many problems and yet so little time to solve them, try to solve at least one. The problem will happen without our direct influence by action or choice, but they will not go away on their own. The secret lies in handling them one by one each day at a time and in learning the secret to avoiding them in the future.

Pick a problem a day and focus on finding a solution to it without dividing your attention. You may want to clear a long-held misunderstanding between yourself and another person, or are you getting very distracted at work? Alternatively, have you struggled with a project, and you want to improve it? Do you have anything in your house that needs fixing? Face the problem and find a solution. To help you solve the problem, here is an example:

Sample Process

This approach will give you a guideline for handling problems that you decide to face daily. The step by step guide will involve the following:

- Define and clearly state the problem as much as you can.

- Take time to study the problem and understand it and what is expected. If you have no control over a certain problem, set them aside and focus on the ones that you can find a solution for.

- Find out the information you need to solve the problem, actively gather all the necessary information to help you solve the problem.

- With keenness, interpret and analyze the information you have collected, pick reasonable and appropriate inferences that you can

- Find out what you can possibly do either shortly or in the long run. Make clear all your options for action, and imagine the solution that seems ideal.

- Analyze your options, taking note of their pros and cons

- Adopt a systematic and strategic approach to the problem and go through with it.

- Observe the results of your action as they emerge and be ready to change your strategy if called upon to do so. Always be prepared to change your strategy, analysis or the statement of the problem and sometimes all the three as you gain more information that may drive to this.

The process of improving critical thinking takes practice and time. Hopefully, the above 5 practices or strategies will be useful to you in improving your critical thinking skills. With practice every day, you improve your skills and critical thinking becomes part of you.

How to Improve Critical Thinking in College and Why It Is Necessary

As earlier discussed, critical thinking has many definitions. Another simplified definition would be the deliberate and systematic processing of data so as to make better decisions and have a better understanding of things. Critical thinking requires the application of diverse intellectual tools to different sets of information.

When you are thinking about information, what ways do you critically look at it?

- Conceptualize
- Analyze
- Synthesize and
- Evaluate

Where will your information come from?

- Observation
- Experience
- Reflection
- Reasoning
- Communication

What is the information meant to do or guide you in?

- Beliefs
- Action

Critical thinking is the opposite of your regular, normal thinking. Most of the time, thinking is automatic. However, when you critically think it means you deliberately or intentionally employ one or more of the above intellectual tools in order to arrive at a more accurate conclusion than you would automatically.

As a college student, you may ask why does it matter to think critically?

True, our thinking is not critical most of the time. If we were to think about every single action critically, we might not have any cognitive energy left to think about the more important things—hence, it is good that we have some automatic thinking. However, we are likely to run into some problems if we allow the automatic mental process to govern or direct important decisions.

Without critical thinking skills, it is possible to be manipulated and for catastrophes of every kind to result. In our day-to-day life, it is easy to be caught up in pointless arguments or say things that you later regret because we failed to take a moment and think deliberately or critically.

So this why critical thinking matters in college. According to the book *The Thinking Student's Guide to College* by Andrew Roberts, students need critical thinking skills because they often adopt the wrong attitude to thinking when faced with difficult questions. Some of these attitudes include:

- Ignorant certainty – this is the belief that all questions have definite correct answers and the only thing to do is find the right source. This is the thinking of most students when they join college because this is what got them through high school coursework. However, in college and in life, there are no straight forward answers to most questions. To advance in college classes, you must critically think about the information you gather.

- Naïve relativism – this is the belief that there is no truth and that all arguments are equal. According to Roberts, once students discover the error of ignorant certainty, this is the view many students adopt. Granted, it is a more critical approach as compared to ignorant certainty, but it is inadequate because it misses the point of critical thinking; it is a less wrong answer, but it is still wrong. An aspect of critical thinking is evaluating how valid arguments on both sides are. A critical think must be willing to accept that some arguments are better than others.

Critical thinking in college is important because of some of the following reasons:

- It enables you to come up with your own opinions and interact with information beyond a superficial level. This is a very important aspect of writing a great essay and having a discussion that is intelligent with your classmates and lecturers. Do not accept everything the textbook says, learn to critique, and ask questions in order to go far.

- Critical thinking allows you to come up with worthwhile arguments that you can back up. This is important if you plan to pursue further studies because critical and original thought is crucial.

- Critical thinking helps you evaluate and analyze your work. This enables you to obtain better grades and develop better mind habits.

Going through college and doing work without critical thinking will not take you very far. Apply these skills and expand your mind and make your work easier.

Critical Thinking in the Real World

The value of critical thinking continues beyond college. In the real world, critical thinking is more important than ever before because of the following reasons:

- Critical thinking enables you to continue intellectually growing even after you graduate from college. Learning is a lifelong commitment. When out of college, you will still encounter new information that may be in your new place of work or in your daily life. The knowledge of how to think critically will help evaluate and use new information more effectively.

- Critical thinking skills will help you make difficult decisions. The ability to think critically through a situation allows you to compare the pros and cons of the options available to you, and it helps you realize you may have more options than you may imagine.

- Critical thinking will help you avoid manipulation. People will obviously try to manipulate you, and if you take things at face value, then you will fall victim of their manipulations. Being a critical thinker, you will critically analyze the information you receive so as to make well-informed decisions and avoid manipulation. Most advertisements are manipulative and can easily lead you to make wrong decisions. With critical thinking skills, you will never fall victim to these manipulations.

- You turn into someone more employable. Most employers do want to hire people with excellent problem-solving skills and not just with academic qualifications. An employer looks for an employee that will bring solutions to many of the challenges in the organization. To get a good job after graduation, you need critical thinking skills.

There are several ways that will help you think more critically and improve your critical thinking skills in your day-to-day life. The following ways will help you improve your thinking on a day-to-day basis.

1) Ask basic questions – it is possible that an explanation can be very complex, hence losing the meaning of the original question. To avoid this, revisit the original questions you set out to solve the problem below are some basic questions that you can ask:

   - What do you know?
   - How do you know it?

- What do you want to disapprove, prove, critique or demonstrate?
- Are you overlooking something?

Some of the best solutions to problems are simple, not complex. Seek simple answers or solutions first.

2) Question Basic assumptions – it is very easy to make a fool out of yourself by not asking some basic questions about your basic assumptions. Some of the greatest innovators are those that took a moment and questioned if everyone's general assumption was right or wrong. Questioning of assumptions is the beginning of innovations. How about the trip you desire to take or the internship you want to get? All these are possible to become a reality when one questions their assumptions and evaluates their beliefs about what is the right thing to do critically.

3) Be attentive to your mental processes – our brains are known to use shortcuts to explain the happenings around us. If we are trying to think critically, the speed at which our thoughts happen in our minds is very fast and may be a disadvantage when we want to think things through critically. The fast way of thinking can be useful in other areas, but in critical thinking, it can be a disaster. A critical thinker must be aware of their cognitive biases and prejudices and how they are able to influence solutions and decisions. Becoming aware of your

biases enables you to be able to think through things critically.

4) Try reversing things – a great way to get out of a jam of a situation is to reverse. This is like the example of a chicken and an egg, wondering which one came first. Try and reverse situations or methodology and even if the reverse isn't true, it can help you find your way again by analyzing the situation more critically.

5) Evaluate existing evidence – when finding a solution to a problem, consider looking at other work that was previously done on the same problem. This may be of tremendous help because there would be no need to solve a problem from scratch when someone else had already set the groundwork. However, it is very important to evaluate this information to avoid reaching the wrong conclusion. Ask some questions about the information that will help you make a decision on the information like:

- Who collected the evidence?
- How did they collect it?
- Why did they collect it?

For example, pick a study showing the advantages of sugary cereal. The information you find may be very good, but once you discover the manufacturer of the cereal funded the research, you automatically know the findings are biased, and so you cannot use them for your research.

6) Think for yourself – thinking for yourself and independently can be a powerful tool. Do not allow yourself to be overconfident but understand that thinking for yourself is very important in answering difficult questions. Do not get lost in other people's work but practice independent thinking.

7) Know that nobody critically thinks all the time – it is not possible to think critically all the time and that is not a problem. The tool that is critical thinking is such that you can deploy it when you require to make critical decisions or solve tough problems. It is also possible to experience lapses in reasoning on important matters, and the solution is to recognize the lapses and try to work towards avoiding them in the future.

It is therefore clear that critical thinking is important both in the classroom and outside of it. Critical thinking is applicable in every area of your life and as such should be practiced every time until it becomes second to nature. Gaining skills in critical thinking and improving them is a lifelong journey because there is always more and new things to learn.

Critical thinking is a lifelong skill. Every day we are learning something new or facing different challenges. These situations if we choose to look at them critically in order to draw the best conclusions, we continuously improve our critical thinking skills. It is possible to forget to apply critical thinking when analyzing the situation, but once you realize it, start again to ensure your judgment is the best based on the information you have.

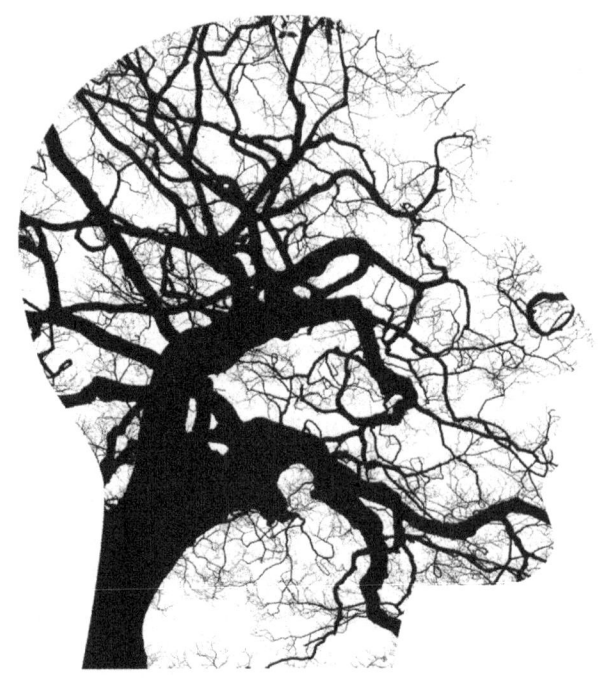

CHAPTER FOUR: TECHNIQUES, STRATEGIES, SKILLS

There are many techniques, strategies, and skills to critical thinking that help you in the process of critical thinking. In this chapter, we shall discuss the different strategies, skills, and techniques, as well as how to use them to enable effective critical thinking in decision-making and problem-solving. Some of the techniques of critical thinking are as follows:

Clarify.

Put down one point at a time, discuss it, and give examples. Ask for clarity and examples from others. If you are not clear and sure of what you are talking about, then you cannot effectively address it. For instance,

Unclear, 'how can we correct the education system?'

Clear, 'how can teachers help students prepare for the students for the workforce?' or 'how can we change policies to improve the quality of education in our schools?

Be accurate.

Always check your facts.

Inaccurate, 'most people are obese these days' or 'just vent the anger, you will feel better.'

Accurate, 'many people are not obese in the US' or 'research shows that letting out your anger increases your anger feelings and actions.'

Be precise.

Being precise helps you check accuracy. Avoid generalizing issues, ambiguity, and euphemisms.

Imprecise, 'Mary is obese.'

Precise, Mary is 10 pounds over her recommended weight based on her body mass index.

Be relevant.

Avoid digressing. Focus on how every idea is connected to the main idea.

Know your purpose.

Separate your main purpose from related purpose. Understand what you are trying to accomplish and what is most important

Identify assumptions.

Every thinking is based on assumptions regardless of how basic it is.

Check your emotions.

Emotions will confuse critical thinking. Establish how your emotions may be directing your thinking in a certain way.

Empathize.

Try and see things in the eyes of your opponent. Try and imagine how they feel, how they perceive you, sympathize and understand their logic, perspective and emotions.

Identify your ignorance.

Every person knows a tiny fraction of all the information in the world. It is possible to be wrong even when you may know more about a certain subject than your opponent. Seek to know more but remain humble.

Be independent.

Think for yourself. Do not accept and believe everything you read, question it. Do not settle for the values, perspectives, or priorities of others. Come up with your own conclusions.

Think through implications.

Think about the consequences of your conclusions. Be certain that the consequences are acceptable

Know your biases.

Your biases will cloud your thinking and judgment. They are likely to direct your thoughts towards a certain end regardless of the logic applied.

Suspend judgment.

Critical thinking is what should result in judgment—not judgment before critical thinking. Never make a decision first and use critical thinking to back up your decision. Critically analyze a situation first then form a judgment after.

Consider the opposition.

Be willing to listen to diverse viewpoints from others. Do not dismiss them; instead, you should seriously consider their persuasive arguments. Avoid being narrow-minded as much as possible and be open-minded instead.

Recognize cultural assumptions.

People from diverse cultures and times are likely to think or reason differently from you. Your ideas may not be the very best or may have developed based on your culture just like for others. Consider all ideas by understanding why they are diverse.

Be fair, not selfish.

Every person has a basic bias to themselves. Accept that you can make mistakes and be the cause of a problem. Do not expect every decision to be in your favor or to what you like but consider it may be better the other way.

Practicing critical thinking using the above techniques will help you develop and improve your skills until critical thinking becomes second to nature for you.

Strategies for Developing Critical Thinking in Students

Critical thinking is an important skill for the modern times. It is about analyzing, questioning and challenging situations as well as issues and information of all types. We use critical thinking skills when we ask questions about theories, conventional wisdom, survey results among others. So what strategies should we use to build these skills in students? The following techniques help students acquire critical thinking skills and have a great impact on their learning.

1) Socratic seminars – these are wonderful tools that facilitate in-depth conversations between students based on a given text. A teacher usually assigns a text to students and asks them to read and prepare for a class discussion. The students discuss amongst themselves, listening to each other with each student participating. The teacher acts as the moderator of the discussion and remains neutral.

2) Simulations – simulations are a great way to encourage critical thinking. Some areas of study come to life as students make decisions as though they are experiencing events first hand. Simulations usually provide a lasting impact on the retention of content.

3) Encourage creativity – instead of giving detailed instructions or directions to students to complete an activity, just make materials required available and step back and let the children use their creativity. It may surprise a teacher how much students can accomplish if left alone to control their own learning.

4) Depth and complexity icons – the in-depth complexity icons that were introduced by Sandra Kaplan that include ethics, details, unanswered questions, trends, rules, languages, big ideas, and disciplines help stimulate in-depth analysis. When used across various levels, they help students think about a subject critically.

5) Compare and Contrast – encourage students to compare and contrast ideas and concepts, theories, objects, and living things. Comparison charts can help in this exercise.

6) Literature circles – allow students to select books that they can present and discuss in the classroom. When they discuss amongst themselves, students get motivated to dig deeper

and critically think about issues presented in the book that on their own they may not have considered.

7) Debates – debates are known to sharpen students' ability or persuasion skills. They are able to persuade a given audience about a particular topic and to do this they need to analyze the information they have on the particular subject critically. Debates also help students to listen and speak articulately of their points actively as well as enhance their critical thinking skills.

8) Instant challenges – this is an excellent way to begin the day in school because the students are forced to think critically and express creativity under pressure. Students work as a team or in groups, complete a given challenge within a short time, and then do a presentation of their work to the class that will judge their performance. This is also a great way to develop and even improve critical thinking skills in students.

9) Open-ended questioning – many students are used to questions that offer only one answer. Give students open-ended questions that will enable them to think at a higher level and will trigger their curiosity to learn more and critically analyze every information they find.

10) Reciprocal Teaching – divide students into small groups with each having a role as a question generator, clarifier, summarizer, or predictor. They can also take turns as

moderator. The aim of reciprocal teaching is to encourage students to get involved in the discussion and deeply think about what they are reading.

How to Teach Critical Thinking in Schools

Critical thinking skills are important skills in our day-to-day lives. Critical thinking skills are important to students too. There are many ways in which a teacher can seek to teach these skills to the students. Critical thinking is not only about clear and rational thinking, but it also involves independent thinking. This means formulating opinions and coming up with unbiased conclusions based on the available information. It calls for discipline in analysis and identifying connections between ideas as well as being open to wide viewpoints and opinions.

To teach critical thinking skills does not require special equipment but rather curious minds with simple strategies.

Teaching Strategies for Critical Thinking Skills

The following techniques will help a teacher in teaching critical thinking skills to students:

1. Begin with questions

   This is the simplest way to start critical thinking lessons. Whatever you want to explore and discuss should not be in the form of questions that require a 'yes" or 'no' answer.

Develop essential questions that create the curiosity for knowledge and problem-solving. When you pose these questions, encourage the students to brainstorm as you list possible answers on the board. Having this kind of an open discussion with students is a great way to collectively identify the problem, analyze the information, and come up with the best solution.

2. Create a foundation

Information is central to any critical thinking exercise. Begin critical thinking exercises with a review of relevant information. This ensures that they are able to remember facts on the topic in discussion. These may come from:

- Reading assignments or home works
- Critical thinking exercises or previous lessons
- A text reading or video

3. Consult the classics

Challenging narratives from great literary works are a perfect way to start critical thinking. Use these works for lessons in plot predictions, motivation, or themes. You can explore things like

- Critical thinking and Shakespeare
- The critical thinking community among others.

4. Creating a country

   This can be a great learning project needing sufficient research to discover what makes a country, and in the process, the students get to learn history, politics, geography, and many more. Leave the assignment as an open-ended exercise for a few days and see what the students come up with.

5. Use information fluency

   Critical thinking as a tool enables you to know when to pursue or discard information. Students must understand how to collect the appropriate information to inform their thinking. Understanding information fluency is key to teaching critical thinking skills to students. Students need to master the correct use of information in order to succeed in their school life. It is about developing the skills to dig through knowledge and finding the most appropriate and useful facts to enable problem-solving.

6. Utilize peer groups

   Because of digitalization, many students excel in environments where critical thinking skills are developed through collaboration and teamwork. Show the students how their peers are excellent sources of knowledge, problem-solving techniques, and questions.

7. Try one sentence

This technique involves an exercise where students are divided into small groups of 5 to 7 students. Next, the students are each instructed to write one sentence describing a topic then the paper is passed to the next student that adds their interpretation of the next step in one sentence but folds down the paper to cover their sentence and so forth. Each time the paper is passed on, the student can only see one sentence. This exercise aims at teaching the students to close in on a specific moment. They also get to learn how to apply knowledge and logic in explaining themselves as much as possible.

8. Problem-solving

This is the best way of teaching critical thinking skills to students. Assign a problem that is open-ended to allow the students to explore and analyze knowledge through critical thinking.

9. Return to roleplaying

This is an excellent way of practicing critical thinking. When actors are given a character to play, they do a lot of research into the character because the role involves taking the persona of the character—hence calling for both creative and analytical mind. Pair students up and assign them to research on a conflict that involves interaction between historical figures. Help them decide what character they will each play—they each have varying points of view on the conflict. Let them analyze it until they can each explain the other's point of view then suggest a compromise.

10. Speaking with sketch

In as much as we are visual learners, it can be challenging to communicate an idea effectively without words. However, the translation of thoughts to picture encourages critical thinking. It guides children using varied mental skill set and for them to get totally invested in the idea.

11. Prioritize it

Every subject presents critical thinking opportunities. Prioritize critical thinking skills in your lessons. Check for understanding and create room for discussion. This practice will start cultivating critical thinking as a way of learning rather than an activity.

12. Change their misconceptions

A lot of work and concentration is involved in critical thinking, but it is best to let students do the process by themselves. However, it can be helpful to step in and help where necessary in order to correct misconceptions or assumptions. Students will richly benefit from critical thinking for better learning in the long run.

There are many techniques that a person can apply to acquire and develop critical thinking skills. Different disciplines may apply different methods, but in all disciplines, the critical thinking process must be applied. Once you understand the process, you can formulate your own ways of acquiring or improving critical thinking as long as you apply the processes. Always remember that the skills of critical thinking are acquired over a period of time through practice.

CHAPTER FIVE: TYPES OF CRITICAL THINKING

The term "critical thinking" is actually incredibly broad. So far, we have discussed it in terms of elements common to several different forms of it, which we covered in chapter four. This chapter will look at the different types of critical thinking.

Logical Reasoning

In its formal sense, logic is a system of rules according to which one may make inferences or draw conclusions. In other words, logic dictates how facts and conditions can be used to gain new understanding.

For example, if we begin with the factual statement that "A beagle is a type of dog," and then add the fact that "Rover is a beagle," we can then conclude that "Rover is a dog." However, if we are told "Scruffy is a dog," the laws of logic do not allow us to conclude that "Scruffy is a beagle." All beagles are dogs, but it does not follow that any dog is a beagle, so we cannot say anything else about Scruffy.

Notice that the logical example above does not show evidence for any of its claims. The facts we started with (a.k.a. "premises") are true for the sake of argument. This is why critical thinking requires evidence as well as logic, to ensure that logical claims reflect reality.

Logic is an entire discipline in itself. For now, we'll cover the three types of logical reasoning that cover most arguments.

- Deductive reasoning or deduction guarantees the truth of a conclusion based on its premises.

All humans are mortal, and Andrew is a human. Therefore, Andrew is mortal.

> It has been established that being human means being mortal, so if we know that Andrew is a human, then we know he is a mortal.

- Inductive reasoning shows something is probable but not definitely true according to its premises.

> August has been the hottest month of the year in this region since we began tracking temperatures, so this year it will probably be the hottest month.

> There is an established record of August being the hottest month during the year, so it is likely the hottest month of them all. Yet there is no scientific law or rule saying it has to be the hottest month, so it is possible that this year another month could be even hotter than August.

Notice that deductive reasoning starts with a general statement—in this case, a statement about all humans—and uses it to reach a specific conclusion, i.e., a conclusion about the specific case of Andrew. On the other hand, inductive uses a specific observation—in this case, what we know about August in the past—to make a general statement that is probable but not necessarily completely true, namely that August is the absolute hottest month of them all.

Scientific Reasoning

The scientific method is the process by which scientists and many other scholars and critical thinkers use tests and experimentation to support a claim. It is a general mode of thinking that—while primarily associated with experiments in the physical sciences such as biology, chemistry, and physics—is also prevalent in the social sciences as well as in philosophy and other disciplines.

The scientific method begins with a specific question, such as "How can I use electricity to power something?" or "Why are people suffering from this disease?" The person wishing to answer their question then provides a "hypothesis," an educated guess that they believe is possible based on what they know already. They will then conduct a test in the form of several experiments or the collection of data relevant to the problem.

They may experiment with different models for harnessing electricity, compare the health records and routines of the patients living in the infected region, or simply try different brands of detergent. They then analyze their findings to draw a conclusion.

Experiments are often replicated to test results under different conditions. For example, if the experimenter found a correlation between people suffering from the same diseases in a certain area and their ingestion of a chemical in the water, they might conduct an experiment on lab animals using those chemicals, or find another population demonstrating a similar correlation and analyze them.

As discussed earlier, no scientific theory is ever concluded to be one-hundred-percent accurate, and no experiment or test can demonstrate the absolute truth of any proposition. That is why scientists and others continue to test, experiment, and then reexamine things so that they can claim an overwhelming likelihood that their conclusion is correct. Evidence may never be perfect but imperfect evidence is not the same as a lack of evidence.

The Psychology of Critical Thinking

Critical thinking in psychology is defined as the habits and skills to engage in activity or exercise with reflection and criticism focusing on deciding what to believe and decisions to make. Critical thinking is a tool that is important even in psychology, and it is being taught in psychology classes. Many students coming to college have already formed theories and opinions of the subject and of life in general. When they are faced with college work, they get a shock when they find it is not what they thought it would be. Some students opt to cram the textbooks so that they will help them in the exams forgetting learning entails more than that.

For these reasons, psychology professors decided to teach critical thinking by approaching it in a systematic, purposeful, and developmental manner. The proposal was to teach critical thinking skills in 3 main domains of psychology: practical (the functionality), theoretical (development of scientific explanations for behaviors), and methodological (testing of scientific ideas).

Practical Domain

Practical critical thinking is expressed as the long-term goal of psychology teachers even as much as they don't spend a lot of time teaching critical skills to students in order to become better consumers or careful judges of character etc. Accurate interpretation of behavior is essential, but few teachers spend time teaching this to students and aiding them in understanding the way their thoughts are not invulnerable.

To instill critical thinking skills in students, encourage the practice of accurate description and behavior by giving students ambiguous tasks for example, as students to differentiate the behavior they observe from the inferences they find out of the behavior. With this exercise, students will discover that behavioral descriptions are consistent between observers, but inferences will vary widely. They realize that how they interpret is biased at times and personal because of their own preferences and values. Because of these strong differences in interpretations, students are likely to learn not to be overly confident about their immediate judgment or conclusions that they need to be more tolerant of ambiguity and be willing to give alternative interpretations as they need a good understanding of procedures in science, effective control skills and legitimate forms of evidence. With these, they will less likely be victims of multiple off-base claims or conclusions about behavior that faces us all.

Theoretical Domain

Theoretical critical thinking is about helping a student develop an appreciation of science in explaining behavior. This means that not only learning the content of psychology but how to organize psychology into concepts and why it is organized into concepts, theories, principles, and laws. Development of skills theoretically starts in the introductory class where the main critical thinking objective is applying and understanding concepts properly. For instance, when students are introduced to the principles of reinforcement, challenge them to find examples of the principles in the news or come up with stories that demonstrate the principles.

Mid-level courses require more advancement where students are moved from the application of concepts to learning how to apply theories. For example, provide a case study that is rich in abnormal psychology, then ask students to interpret and make sense of it from different perspectives by making use of accepted and existing frameworks in psychology to explain behavior patterns.

In advanced levels, students can be asked to evaluate theory rejecting the least helpful or selecting the most useful. For instance, students can argue different models to discuss drug addiction in physiological psychology by evaluating the weaknesses and strengths of existing frameworks. They can choose the theories that work best by justifying their conclusions based on reason and evidence.

Graduate and honors courses go beyond the evaluation of theory and encourage students to create or come up with original theories. Students choose a difficult question on behavior and build their own theory-based explanations to the behavior. This kind of challenge requires them to synthesize and include exiting theory as well as come up with new insights into the behavior.

Methodological Domain

Many departments give opportunities for students to build their methodological critical thinking skills by applying varied research methods in psychology. Beginner students first learn what the scientific method involves. The next step will be applying their own understanding of the scientific method by identifying elements in existing research. For example, a detailed description of experimental design will help a student practice differentiating the dependent from the independent variable and understanding how researchers controlled for different explanations.

The next critical thinking in methodology goals includes evaluating the quality of existing research and critiquing the conclusions of the research findings. Students may require encouragement from the teachers to overcome fear they sometimes experience for anything printed even their textbooks. Asking students to carry out a critical analysis on a sophisticated design may be too much for them to undertake. They are likely to do much better when given assignments from bad designs so that they can cultivate critical abilities as well as the confidence to handle more complex designs. After this, students will be able to develop their own research designs in their methodology courses. When you ask students to run their own independent research be it a comprehensive study on parental attitudes, a well-thought experiment on paired-associate studying or a study on the behavior of a museum patron, it makes students use their critical thinking skills and gives them an opportunity to practice with conventional writing in psychology.

After the students complete their work, ask them to evaluate the strengths and weaknesses of their work as this will help them in developing their critical thinking skills.

There are many ways and areas critical thinking and reasoning can be applied. Different disciplines and areas of life require the application of critical thinking processes in order to form the best decision and conclusions.

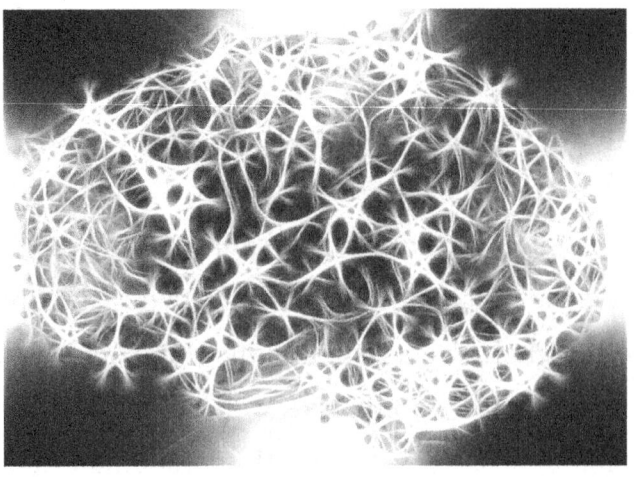

CHAPTER SIX: EXERCISES FOR CRITICAL THINKING

Time to Think Critically

Critical thinking is a process—not an easy fix. It takes time and thought. Think of the time and thought as an investment in making the right decision.

You may want to write out that process. You might think about it all in your head. Either way, critical thinking involves organizing one's thoughts so that they can be adapted around the facts at hand. It also involves ensuring that they are your thoughts— aligned with facts and logic—rather than assumptions handed down to you. It may sound like a lengthy process, but the more you do it, the easier and more intuitive it will become.

Start by Asking How You Will Make Your Decision

What does "the best car" mean? What would "the right candidate" do? What does "help" mean when you say you want to help a friend? It is important to understand the topic, question, issue, or choice in front of you on your terms. For example, you might want a car that looks nice. You might think a political leader should concentrate on keeping crime down (while another voter might prioritize the environment or another issue).

Ask yourself why you want those things. Would a nice-looking car be there for you to admire it, or to impress other people? Is crime that big of a problem in your community, or is that just something that everyone around you seems to concentrate on?

Before you even begin to make a decision, be honest about what you are looking for as a result of that decision. Along the way, you may even change your mind. Maybe you realize that you don't want to spend as much money on a fancy car just so that other people can admire it. Perhaps you learn that the crime rate is much lower than you thought, but there is another immediate, more pressing issue affecting you. The point is to understand why we do the things we do and to be honest about motives. Critical thinking requires objectivity, even when it comes to ourselves.

Who, and How, Do You Trust Anything?

Now that you have accurately established what is important to you in approaching this issue, you can start gathering the facts. A "fact," in broad terms, is an event or action that is known to have taken place, a thing that is verified as existing in the world, or a piece of information or occurrence that has been verified either through observation, experience, experimentation, or some other evidence-based process. In other words, facts are true according to some verifiable standard.

Whenever you are presented with a piece of information, such as a description of a car's features or of a political candidate's agenda, first consider the tone of the language. Is it overly favorable or unfavorable? Does it present things in neutral terms, or does it use excessively colorful or negative language? Does it stick to descriptive statements, or does it make inferences for you? In other words, is the language there to educate you, or is the language trying to "sell you" something?

Next, consider the source of that information. Is that source speaking from their own experience, or are they just basing off the information they've gathered from elsewhere? Does the source have anything to gain, for example in terms of profit or popularity, by Does it come from a well-known source, such as a major political newspaper, or a website you have never heard of? Popular sources can get things wrongs, and lesser-known sources can get the scoop on things before famous ones, but generally, those well-known sources are well-known because they have established a reputation for reliability.

Analyzing Facts and Applying Logic

Hopefully, you will have collected enough facts to help you make a decision. The process of applying facts to the issue at hand is called "analysis." Ensuring that the facts are consistent with each other and drawing conclusions from the involves "logic." Philosophers, mathematicians, psychologists, and other scholars all have vastly sophisticated systems to describe and outline analysis as well as logic. For the purposes of this book, we will stick to less abstract, more "on-the-ground" examples of analysis and logic.

What do the facts tell us in relation to the questions and definitions we raised earlier? What do we now know about the safety of the car we want to purchase or the candidate's plan for decreasing crime? It may not always be a cut and dried answer to those questions. Everything the candidate says may indicate that he is tough on crime. Yet the policies he has enacted in the past indicate the contrary. Based upon how the candidate has acted in the past, and despite his other rhetoric, it is safe to assume he will not be tough on crime. This assumption is an "inference," a logical deduction based on some form of evidence. We will discuss different types of logical reasoning later on in this book.

Note that an assumption based on suitable evidence is very different than an assumption based upon unproven claims, bias, or shoddy evidence. Scientific theories, for example, make use of the best evidence and experimentation possible, but no scientific theory is ever proven to be one-hundred-percent accurate. That would mean the theory has been tested under all possible circumstances accounting for all variables possible in the universe, even the ones we haven't encountered yet! However, "it could be wrong" is not the same thing as "it is wrong." Remember that something with a ninety-percent chance of being true is very different than something with a fifty-percent chance, and the polar opposite of a claim that offers no evidence.

You can never be certain that a source is completely accurate or totally unbiased. Critical thinking involves using the best possible information from the most reliable sources to make a decision or judgment.

Critical Thinking Exercises

Critical thinking is the suspension of your beliefs in order to explore and question topics from a neutral or blank point of view. It also calls for the ability to differentiate a fact from opinion when evaluating a topic.

Have you ever wanted to analyze and evaluate situations like a master detective? Or even present arguments like a seasoned lawyer yet you are not one? Are you tired of seeming confused and out of place in intellectual forums or in class or in life in general?

Critical thinking is what will help you out of this mess. Critical thinking is a skill, an art and a practice that gets to the core of any subject allowing you to see the bigger picture and challenge and critique whatever comes between the truth and you.

Critical thinking, however, does not come easy. It requires to be developed and practiced before it becomes second to nature to any person. To develop it further, it requires critical thinking exercises and practices.

There are many exercises that can help a person develop critical thinking skills. In this part, we shall discuss a few of them.

Critical Thinking for Students

Exercise 1: Alien tour guide

This exercise is an attempt to get the students to think outside the box.

Assume you have been tasked to conduct a tour for aliens who have visited earth and want to understand human life. You are riding in a blimp as you view the scenes and landscape below. You find yourselves passing over a baseball stadium. One of the visiting aliens looks down and is curious about what is going on. You tell him that there is a game going on. Assuming he asks you the following questions, how would you answer him?

- What is a game?
- Why is it only played by males? There are no female players?
- Why do people seem so excited when they watch others play games?
- What is a team?

- Why are there some people on the seats and others on the field?

If you answer these questions comprehensively, it will become clear that we carry around assumptions and values. There are reasons that you support a certain team—maybe it makes you feel like part of a community. The sense of community in itself is a value that matters to some people and not to others. You may also need to explain to the alien the value of winning and losing. When you reason like an alien tour guide, you will find yourself thinking deeply into the things we do and value, and you may be shocked if they don't sound logical to them.

Exercise 2: Opinion or fact

Are you always able to differentiate fact from opinion? If you do not learn the difference between facts and opinions, you will only be reading and watching things that enhance assumptions and beliefs that you already have.

In this exercise, try and determine whether the statement sounds like an opinion or a fact and discuss with a classmate.

- My mom is the only best mom on earth
- My dad is a lot taller than your dad
- My telephone number is hard to memorize
- The deepest part of the ocean is 35,913 feet in depth
- Dogs are better pets than turtles

- Smoking is harmful to your health
- More than 80% of lung cancer cases in the U.S. are as a result of smoking
- When you flatten and pull out a slinky toy, it will stretch to be 88 feet long
- Slinky toys are funny
- One in every 100 American citizens is color blind
- Two out of every 10 Americans are boring

You will realize at the end of the exercise that some statements are easy to judge while others are difficult. If you are able to debate how true some statements are, then they are probably opinions.

Critical Thinking Exercises in the Workplace

One of the fundamental skills a leader or manager must have is critical thinking skills. These skills are essential for problem-solving in the organization, dealing with your employees, dealing with your clients, dealing with your business environment like competitors or even helping you when coming up with a new product. There are several critical thinking exercises that can help improve your critical thinking skills in the workplace. These include:

Exercise 1: Analyze your competitors

Study your competitors, try and describe their strategies and most important how where and how they make money. Try and discover which are their customer focus groups, how and why they win or lose. Now come back and analyze your own organization based on the same. Identify the opportunities your organization has over the competition and how to use these opportunities to win over them. Involve your customer care colleagues or your salespeople in the exercise and gain their opinion on the competitor strategies and opportunities. Analyze every information critically and objectively and find a solution. Maybe your problem was how to increase sales, use the information you have gathered to come up with strategies that will increase sales in your organization.

Exercise 2: Identify and adopt an orphan problem

There are problems in every organization that people do not want to be associated with. Identify such a problem and request for your boss's help in handling it. If it is an issue affecting different departments, you may need to gather a team with members from different departments. Guide the team through analyzing the problem, interview all stakeholders and purpose to develop a solution that is informed. As you do this, you gain visibility as a problem solver and a leader as well as develop your core professional skills.

Powerful Skills Related to Critical Thinking

Critical thinking is centered within the three powerful skills of linking ideas, recognition of incongruences and structural arguments. Each area must be practiced and applied in order to develop to a great critical thinker. These skills for critical thinking are:

- Linking ideas – this is about finding a connection or a relation between unrelated or irrelevant with the relevant or relatable.
- Structuring arguments – putting together the elements or aspects that necessary in creating a relevant, practical sound argument.
- Recognizing incongruences – this is the ability to find inconsistencies or holes in any theory or argument in search of the real truth.

Linking ideas

Exercise: Newspaper link up

Take a days' newspaper, scan through all the articles from news, to sports, to business, etc., write up a list of these articles as a basic concept. Now try to identify ways in which each article could be linked to the other in each section. Identify the overall theme in each section and if possible, link the sections of the newspaper to each other. After this, try and summarize the aim of the newspaper.

Structuring arguments

As you begin this exercise, it is of importance to understand the difference between the premise and the conclusion for any argument.

Premise – it is a statement that has been made before or a proposition from which another statement is referenced or follows as a conclusion. It is the base of an undertaking, theory or an argument.

Conclusion – it is the end of an argument, an undertaking or a theory. It is also defined as a judgment or decision reached by reasoning.

Exercise: Recognizing the premise and the conclusion

Search through YouTube or Google some theories, speeches or arguments that have ever been done or given. Take the piece you chose and try and identify the premise of the topic and the conclusion of the topic. It is possible to have several premises, but they must support the conclusion.

Recognizing incongruences

Exercise – Challenging the premise

Pick the same data from the recognizing premise and conclusion activity above, try and figure out if there is a premise that does not support the conclusion. If all premises link to the conclusion, then evaluate the premises themselves and see if there are any fallacies and analyze their validity. Analyze the premises to ensure that there are no statements assumed to be true when they are indeed false.

It is clear that critical thinking is an acquired skill that you can only get if you intentionally purpose to get it. The only sure way of gaining critical thinking skills is through practice. Improving critical thinking skills also requires more practice. Look at every situation that you find yourself in need of applying critical thinking as an exercise and try to find its solution by applying the critical thinking skills discussed previously.

CHAPTER SEVEN: CRITICAL THINKING VERSUS NON-CRITICAL THINKING

What Is NOT Critical Thinking

To help define critical thinking further, let's examine what critical thinking is NOT:

- It's not making snap decisions based on impulse. Knee-jerk reactions are not examples of critical thinking. And neither are habits (even the good ones, though you may have developed those good habits due to critical thinking).
- It's not believing or doing something based entirely on someone in a position of authority telling you to do it. Again, that authority may have important or useful things to say, but it can't be critical thinking if you're not actually thinking about why you do it.
- It's not reacting to situations or judging things based on emotions. If you think you might make a different choice after taking some time to calm down or after a good night's sleep, chances are you are not thinking critically.
- It's not analyzing an issue according to personal bias or assumptions. Statements beginning with "Everyone knows

that…" are usually based on an assumption rather than facts.

- It's not agreeing or disagreeing with a statement based on the speaker's political or cultural background, demeanor, looks, or other personal qualities. Someone may look or sound strange to you, or you may not agree with their political party, but that does not mean every statement they make is incorrect. Similarly, people who look like you or belong to the same associations as you can make incorrect statements.

As you can see, critical thinking is based upon facts, objectivity, and your own independent analysis. We live in an age where we are constantly being bombarded with instructions and information from a variety of sources about everything—from who to vote for to how we should look. Neither the information or its sources are all necessarily accurate or objective, so it is up to you to assess the information around you to find the most precise, unbiased information to help you critically think when making a choice or a judgment.

Background of Critical Thinking

Many scholars trace critical thinking back to the ancient Greek philosopher Socrates, who engaged in long, rigorous discussions with people around him, questioning some of his fellow Athenians' deepest-held beliefs regarding politics and religion.

Through penetrating argument, Socrates forced people to justify their views, and those people often came up short in terms of explanations for why they believed the things that they did.

The tradition of examining claims to find a rational, demonstrable (i.e., containing evidence) justification extended from Socrates through his students Plato and Aristotle to medieval scholastic thinkers such as Aquinas and St. Augustine to the Enlightenment with thinkers such as Kant and Hegel. Yet far from remaining a scholarly method for academic philosophers, critical thinking has shaped the entire modern world, from advances in science and technology to our ethical and political views.

Differences Between Critical Thinking and Ordinary Thinking

Some dictionaries define critical thinking as the analysis and evaluation of a problem objectively in order to form an objective judgment. Most of the time, we are unconscious of the thoughts in our minds. Ordinary thinking usually happens when you are not conscious or attentive. The mind scatters in thought with your attention being in different locations. When you are critically thinking, your attention is more focused consciously and intentionally on a specific area. When you experience anything more consciously, you gain more insight into the particular experience. Our understanding grows much faster when we are conscious. When you focus on a certain area, all the information you will gain will be for that area. In a nutshell, critical thinking is about greater awareness, presence, consciousness and intentional direct focus.

In normal thinking, however, presence or awareness is not very high to enable you to have a silent mind. At this level of thinking, you are unconscious of your thoughts, yet in critical thinking, there is increased awareness, and as a result, it leads to increased knowledge about the area of focus and your understanding on the area increases. This means, you will have more developed thoughts or greater wisdom on the subject, and this is usually the ultimate goal in critical thinking.

Ordinary thinking is the state of mind that is most commonly found in the world. The common person is usually semiconscious and not focused on a certain area. The traits of ordinary that are commonly found are:

- Ordinary level of awareness
- Ordinary level of consciousness
- Ordinary level of presence
- Subconsciously directed attention or focus.

As you advance in the knowledge of the full depth of yourself, you will in due time start transcending towards critical thinking. As you come to the realization of your true nature, your focus will be more towards the experience of critical thinking. You start developing greater inner silence, creativity, and intelligence even during your normal state of mind. The habit of your mind jumping from one thought to the next will reduce, and to more advanced thinkers, it will cease.

Your objective analysis begins to transform, and your mental analysis naturally transforms into inner peace. Your subconscious way of ordinary semi-conscious thinking starts to transform into liberty from patterns into the internal creative being that you are thus the subconscious directed focus is settled and established into your higher self-experiences.

There are some obvious differences between ordinary thinkers and critical thinkers, which are:

- An ordinary thinker accepts information as it is, does not question it, examine or analyze it while a critical thinker does not accept information at face value, he will question, analyze and critique it before using it.
- A critical thinker takes time and does not form conclusions fast, and is aware of the alternatives while a normal thinker accepts the information as factual, does not seek alternatives and uses the information as it is to form conclusions.
- Ordinary thinker never questions or challenge beliefs neither seek evidence while critical thinkers ask

questions, analyze the arguments and assess the facts as they challenge the beliefs.

- Critical thinkers are skillful, active and apply principles of thinking that are necessary to get the truth, unlike ordinary thinkers that are not guided by any principles of thinking.

Characteristics of Critical Thinkers

Critical thinkers are the people that think clearly, objectively and rationally while finding logical connections between ideas. This is a very important skill in exploring and trying to understand the world we live in.

Critical thinking is not all about the gathering of facts, but it is a way of looking at whatever is occupying your mind presently so as to arrive at the best judgment or conclusion. Critical thinkers constantly upgrade or improve their knowledge and take part in self-learning—they make excellent leaders because they are capable of getting to new and high levels of self-improvement as well as self-actualization.

If your aim is to get to your full potential and make a mark in the world, acquire the following characteristics or traits of a critical thinker

1. Observation

    This is one of the first critical thinking skill you learn as a
    child. It is your ability to see and understand the world
    around you. A more detailed observation includes the ability
    to write down details and collect data through senses. Your
    observations will, in the long run, lead to insight and a better
    understanding of the world.

2. Curiosity

    This is a very fundamental trait of some of the most
    successful leaders. Being inquisitive and interested in what is
    happening around you or the people around you is a trait in
    many critical thinkers. A curious person does not take
    anything at face value but will wonder why something is the
    way it is. Curiosity enables you to be open-minded and directs
    you to gain more knowledge, which is important for a critical
    thinker.

3. Objectivity

    Objectivity while looking at information is an important trait
    in a critical thinker. You must focus on the scientific
    evaluation and facts of the information you have. When you
    are an objective thinker, you keep your emotions as well as
    those of others from affecting or influencing your judgment in
    any way. However, it is not easy to stay completely objective.

We are all influenced by our own viewpoints, perspectives, and experiences in life. In order for you to be objective, you must be aware of your biases and look at issues dispassionately. When you successfully are able to get yourself out of a situation, then you be able to analyze it better.

4. Introspection

This is the ability to be able to think about how you think or being consciously away from how you think. Introspection is important to critical thinkers to enable them to be aware of their level of attentiveness and alertness of their thoughts as well as their biases. It is the ability to evaluate your deepest and innermost thoughts, sensations and feelings. This ability is closely related to self-reflection that gives you understanding into your mental state and emotions.

5. Analytical thinking

The best critical thinkers are analytical thinkers, and the best analytical thinkers are the best critical thinkers. In critical thinking, the ability to critically evaluate information on anything or about anything be it a relationship, report or a contract very important. Analysis of information means breaking down information into components and examining how the different parts work separately and together. Analysis depends on observation, collecting and evaluating evidence so as to have an informed conclusion. To be analytical, you must start by being objective.

6. Identifying biases

Critical thinkers must always challenge themselves to know the evidence that helps form their beliefs and assess the credibility of those sources. When you do this, it will help you question your notions and understand your biases.

Knowing and understanding your biases is important because you become aware of how biases influence your thinking and how the information you have collected may also be skewed. As you collect information, you must ask yourself who stands to benefit from that information, if the source of information biased, and if it omits or overlooks details that don't support its notions or claims.

7. Determining relevance

Figuring out what information is most relevant, important and meaningful for your consideration is one of the most difficult parts of critical thinking. In many cases, you may be brought for information that seems valuable but may end up being only a small point to consider.

A critical thinker will check if the information is relevant logically to the issue at hand, if it is useful and unbiased or if it is a distraction from a more important point.

8. Inference

Information most often comes in its raw form. This means that it does not come with a summary that guides you on exactly what it entails. Critical thinkers analyze and draw conclusions and judgment based on raw data. The ability to extrapolate meaning from raw data and discover possible outcomes when evaluating a scenario is what is called inference.

An inference is different from assumptions. For instance, if you find data that says a person weighs 250 pounds, you can assume they are overweight. However, you may come across other data that points out the person is well within their recommended weight because of their height and body composition.

9. Compassion and empathy

Compassion and empathy may seem as negative traits for critical thinkers because they are emotional traits that can influence the situation or its outcome. However, the reason for having compassion is to have concern for others and value their welfare. Lack of compassion will make you view every situation and information from the point of cold data and scientific facts. Looking at situations without compassion may make it easy to allow your cynicism to be toxic and become suspicious of every information you have. A good critical thinker takes into account the human element in situations because everything you do is not about detached information or data.

10. Humility

This is the ability to acknowledge your own shortcomings and see the positive attributes of others objectively and accurately. Humility enables you to be aware of your weaknesses as well as your strengths. For critical thinkers, humility is a very important element that helps them to be able to stretch and be open-minded. With intellectual humility, you are open-minded about other people's viewpoints, acknowledge when wrong, and are flexible to change your beliefs when called upon to.

11. Willingness to change the status quo

In business, critical thinking means questioning business practices that have long been established and refusing to conform to traditional methods with the excuse that it is how things have always been done. Critical thinkers are in search of thoughtful and smart methods and answers that include every relevant practice and information available. Challenging the status quo may not be viewed favorably, but a creative and innovative mind is an integral part of a critical thinker.

12. Open-mindedness

This is the ability of a critical thinker to be able to step back from a situation and see a broader view without being attached to the situation. Critical thinkers do not take sides or jump into conclusions. They are open-minded in how they approach a situation and are able to embrace the viewpoints of others.

13. Aware of common thinking errors

A critical thinker will never allow logic and reasoning to be tainted by illusions and misconceptions. They are consciously aware of logical fallacies which are mistakes in reasoning that find their way into debates and arguments. Some of the common fallacies in thinking are:

- Circular reasoning where the start of the argument or its conclusion is used to support the same argument.

- Cognitive shortcut bias is where you refuse to change from a favored argument or view regardless of the availability of other possibilities that are more effective.

- Confusing correlation with causation is where you assume that when two things happen together, one must be the cause for the other even without evidence. This assumption is not justified.

14. Creative thinking

Critical thinkers are also creative thinkers. Creative thinkers reject problem-solving in a standardized manner and prefer to think outside the box. They have many interests and multiple viewpoints to a problem. They are also open-minded and like to experiment with different methods when solving a problem.

The difference between creative thinkers and critical thinkers is that creative thinkers generate a lot of ideas while critical thinkers analyze and evaluate the ideas. Creativity is important as it brings a variety of ideas while critical thinking will focus on the ideas and analyze them in order to pick the best idea to solve a problem or to draw conclusions on.

15. Effective communicators

Effective communication is characterized by a clear thought process. Most problems in communication are based upon an inability to critically think through a situation or see it through varied viewpoints. Critical thinking is the tool we use to build our thoughts and express them coherently. A good critical thinker must be able to communicate their ideas in a convincing way and internalize the responses of others.

16. Active listeners

To be a good critical thinker, you must be a good active listener. Critical thinkers engage in active listening because they also use other people's viewpoints to form conclusions. They participate in a conversation and avoid being passive. They ask questions in order to avoid assumptions, they collect information and seek to gain knowledge by asking open-ended questions that enable them to dig deeper into the issue.

Eating Habits That Boost Your Critical Thinking

The ability to have critical thinking skills is very important when running a business or an organization and also in your day-to-day life. Many people never think about it, but the food choices you make do affect your critical thinking skills and determine if you are able to make sound decisions. There is no medicine that makes you a great critical thinker, but there are foods that will help boost your brain health and increase your ability to think critically. There are simple diet changes that if adopted will help keep your critical thinking skills sharp helping you have the best performance.

1) Take coffee but moderately.

Caffeine makes you alert but does not give you energy. It is a stimulant that has been associated with increasing thinking ability and attention. The researches that have been carried out on the effects of caffeine to your thinking have been done using 200 to 300 milligrams of caffeine about the same amount found in a cup of coffee. If you take more caffeine than that, your thinking is likely to be negatively affected. Excessive consumption of caffeine will cause anxiety, rambling thoughts, and slurred speech. Make sure you eat something alongside your coffee and avoid more than two cups.

2) Forget the sugar.

A lot of sugar will give you a sugar high, and after about an hour, the buzz drops and your thinking ability goes down as well—hence experiencing a crush. Simple carbs are digested easily, spike your energy levels and blood sugar then soon after it drops like a rock. When it drops, your brain's function and ability to remember is affected negatively.

Limit your intake of sugary food in your diet, and train your body to consume healthier foods. Combine any sugar intake with protein and fiber. Proteins slow down digestion—hence protecting you from abnormal blood sugar surges, while fiber helps slow down the rate at which sugar is absorbed in the bloodstream. If you crave something sweet, take an organic Honeycrisp apple. Eat raw veggie sticks before your meals and increase fiber in your diet.

3) Go nuts.

Studies have shown that seeds and nuts help keep the brain in good shape as well as being a good source of vitamin E associated with reduced cognitive decline. Of particular, walnuts have been found to improve inferential reasoning skills that are fundamental to critical thinking.

4) Do not overeat.

Overdoing things will always backfire. Overeating during lunchtime, for example, can keep you from clear thinking. Overeating leads to decreased blood flow to your brain because it is busy with digestion. Never skip meals but keep them at reasonable portions, eat only when hungry and slow your time of eating.

Obstacles to Creative Thinking and Overcoming Them

Ever felt like your mind is not working, like you can't solve a basic problem? There are several obstacles to creative thinking that may be obstructing you from improving your problem-solving skills. In order to overcome them, you must first recognize them. Some of these obstacles include:

1) Lack of Direction from Others and Yourself

Lack of clearly defined goals and objectives is the first obstacle to critical thinking. Your goals and objectives must be clearly written down together with detailed plans of action. When you are completely clear about what you need and the way to go about it, your creative mind becomes alive. You immediately start generating ideas and insights that help you improve your critical thinking skills.

2) Being Afraid of Failure

Fear of failure or loss is the second obstacle to creative thinking. Many people are afraid of being wrong or making mistakes and even losing money or time. The anticipation and possibility of failure paralyze action and becomes a major reason for ineffective problem solving and failure. Build confidence is using the skill of critical analysis where you are sure that the information you have will lead to an informed conclusion.

3) Being Afraid of Rejection

The fear of criticism, rejection, ridicule or scorn is the third major obstacle to critical thinking. The fear of sounding stupid or looking foolish makes one backtrack on critically thinking through. This is as a result of the desire to feel approved, liked and so forth even by people you don't know. You decide because you want to get along, you then must go along with their findings. Many people live lives of mediocrity or underachievement because they are afraid to be judged or rejected; hence, they cannot bring themselves to sell their ideas. Because of this fear, they play safe and settle for far less than they believe in.

4) Never Changing or Adapting to the Situation

Homeostasis is the subconscious desire to stay and remain consistent with the things you have said or done in the past. This is a major obstacle in critical thinking. It is the fear of suggesting something new or different from your previous suggestions. This impulse holds a person back from achieving success. You find comfort in doing what you have always done, and you get stuck. All progress stops, and you start rationalizing why you are not changing. Homeostasis is a major killer to critical thinking and creative thinking.

5) Not Thinking Proactively

Another obstacle to critical thinking is passivity. If you decide not to stimulate your mind with new information and ideas, it loses its energy and vitality. Instead of thinking critically, proactively and creatively continuously, you become automatic and passive in your thinking. Routine is a major cause of passive thinking. When you follow the same routine every day in doing things, your mind is never challenged to find new ways of doing things. When you don't challenge your mind, it becomes complacent and dull. If a person proposes a new way of doing things, you will react with discouragement and negativity, and you start feeling threatened by any suggestion of change.

6) You Rationalize and Never Improve

Rationalizing is another major obstacle to creative thinking. As rational creatures, we always use our minds to explain the world to ourselves in order to feel more secure and understand it better. This means you always come up with quick explanations as to why you have done or not done something. When you constantly rationalize what you decide, you will not improve your performance.

For instance, as an entrepreneur, there are two main reasons why critical thinking is important to you. The first one is problem-solving and decision-making. At least more than

50% of your time as an entrepreneur is spent solving problems. Becoming a critical thinker as well as a creative thinker will help you in your day-to-day problem-solving abilities that will be inevitable. These skills will enable you to become more successful in your business.

Secondly, we all want to make more money. Your problem-solving abilities are also important in determining how much money you will make.

Critical Thinking Habits of the Mind

There are seven habits that form the mindset of a critical thinker at all times. These habits include:

- Truth-seeking – a critical thinker has intellectual integrity and a desire to strive for the best and factual knowledge as much as possible.

- Open-minded – a critical thinker has a tolerant mindset to divergent views and sensitive to their own biases.

- Analytical – a critical thinker's mind is habitually alert and vigilant to potential problems and consequences that may be short-term or long-term as a result of decisions made or actions taken.

- Systematic – the mindset of a critical thinker is that of organization and order in their approach to solving problems. They are persistent, orderly, focused and diligent.

- Confident in reasoning – their mindset is that of truthfulness in their own reasoning skills in order to yield good judgment.

- Inquisitive – their mindset is that of learning. They habitually strive to be informed; they are naturally curious about how things work and seeking new information every day.

- Judicious – a critical thinker has cognitive maturity and realizes all questions are not as they seem, nothing is black or white, and judgment may sometimes be made in the context of uncertainty.

Here, you have learned why critical thinking is different from ordinary thinking and how it is much more advantageous to approach issues or problems from the point of critical thinking in order to get the best conclusions. Look at the characters of a critical thinker and try to develop the same characters in your thinking. Then, see how much better problem solving will become for you!

Conclusion

Thank you for making it to the end of this e-book, *Critical Thinking*. We hope that it was informative and able to provide you with all of the tools you need to achieve your goals—whatever they may be. This book has been written for every person that has found it difficult to make decisions from time to time and wants skills that will improve their decision-making abilities.

Critical thinking is one of the most important skills that a person needs to acquire in order to go through life more smoothly. Every day of your life, you are faced with the need to make decisions—they can range from what food to eat or what clothes to wear to what decision will be more productive in your place of work.

It is time that you embark on the journey of acquiring and developing critical thinking skills. Stop making rushed decisions or making decisions for the sake of it and later on regretting the decisions you made. Critical thinking is a learned skill, and you must make a conscious decision to develop it. Many times, you will still make mistakes in the decisions you make—that should not discourage you. It is a learning process because the skills are not acquired overnight, but the good news is that if you can commit, then you can learn them and apply them to your day-to-day life. Take your first step today towards consciously learning these skills, and see how things start transforming for the better.

Finally, if this book was of use to you in any way, a review on Amazon is always appreciated!

Made in the USA
Coppell, TX
02 January 2020